Divine Doggos - A Photobook

An Artistic Journey into the World of Canine Charisma

AF256659

By Photopydia

*"Dogs are better than human beings because they know
but do not tell."*

— *Emily Dickinson*

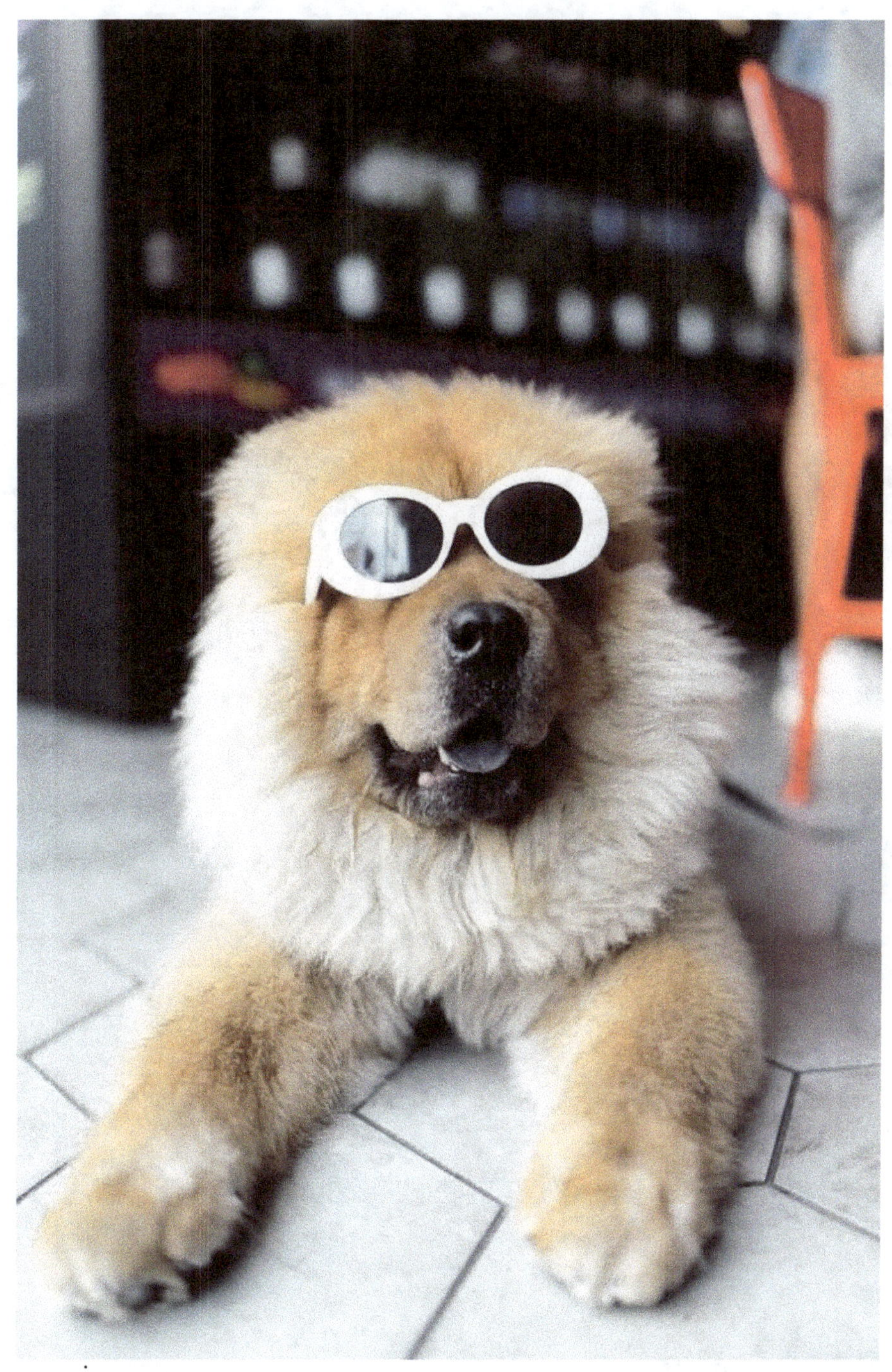

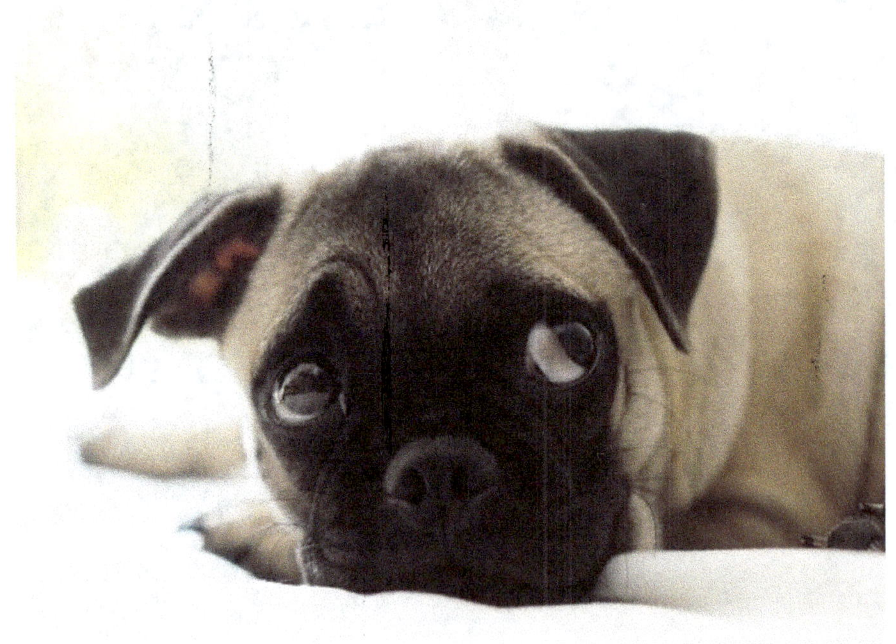

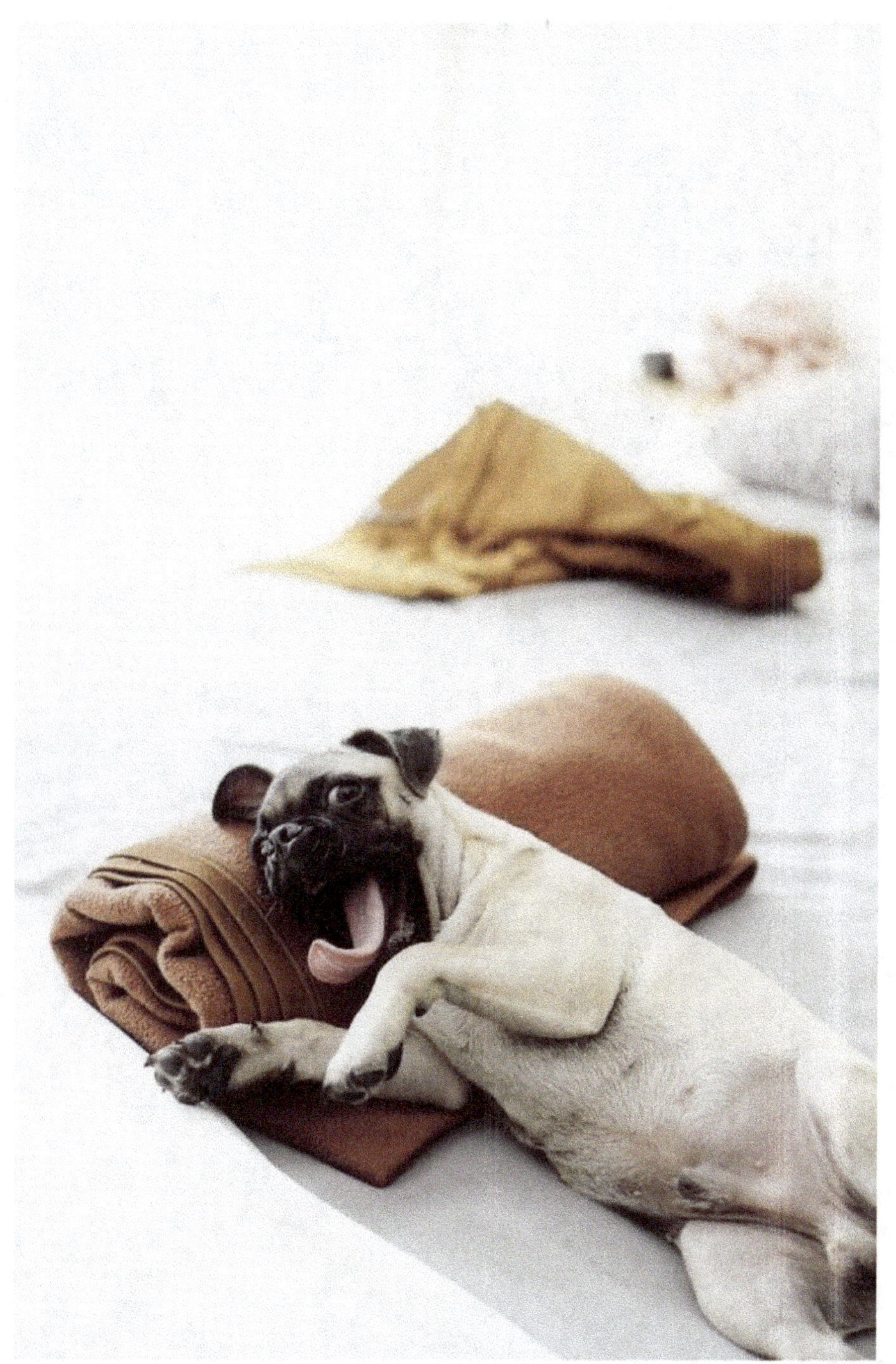

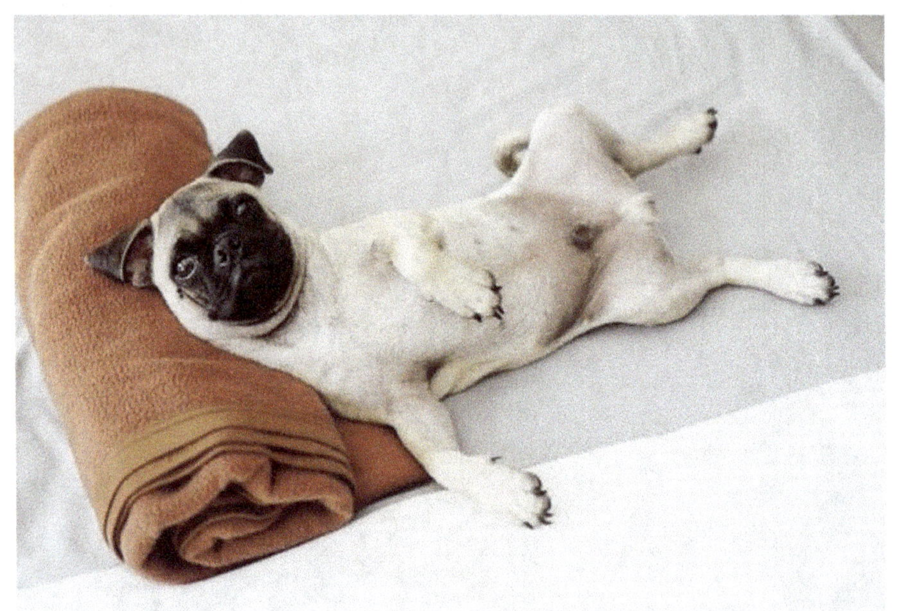

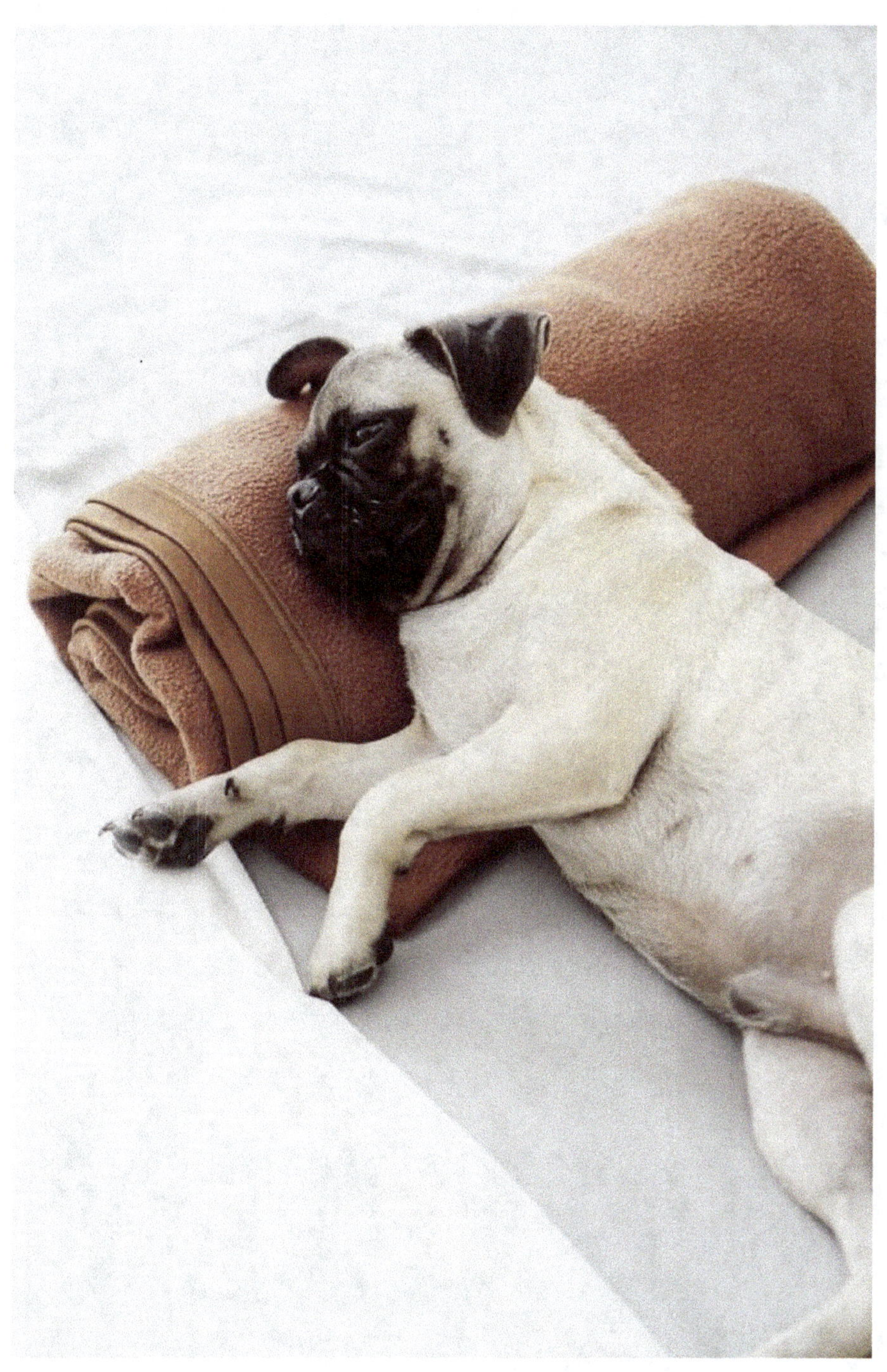

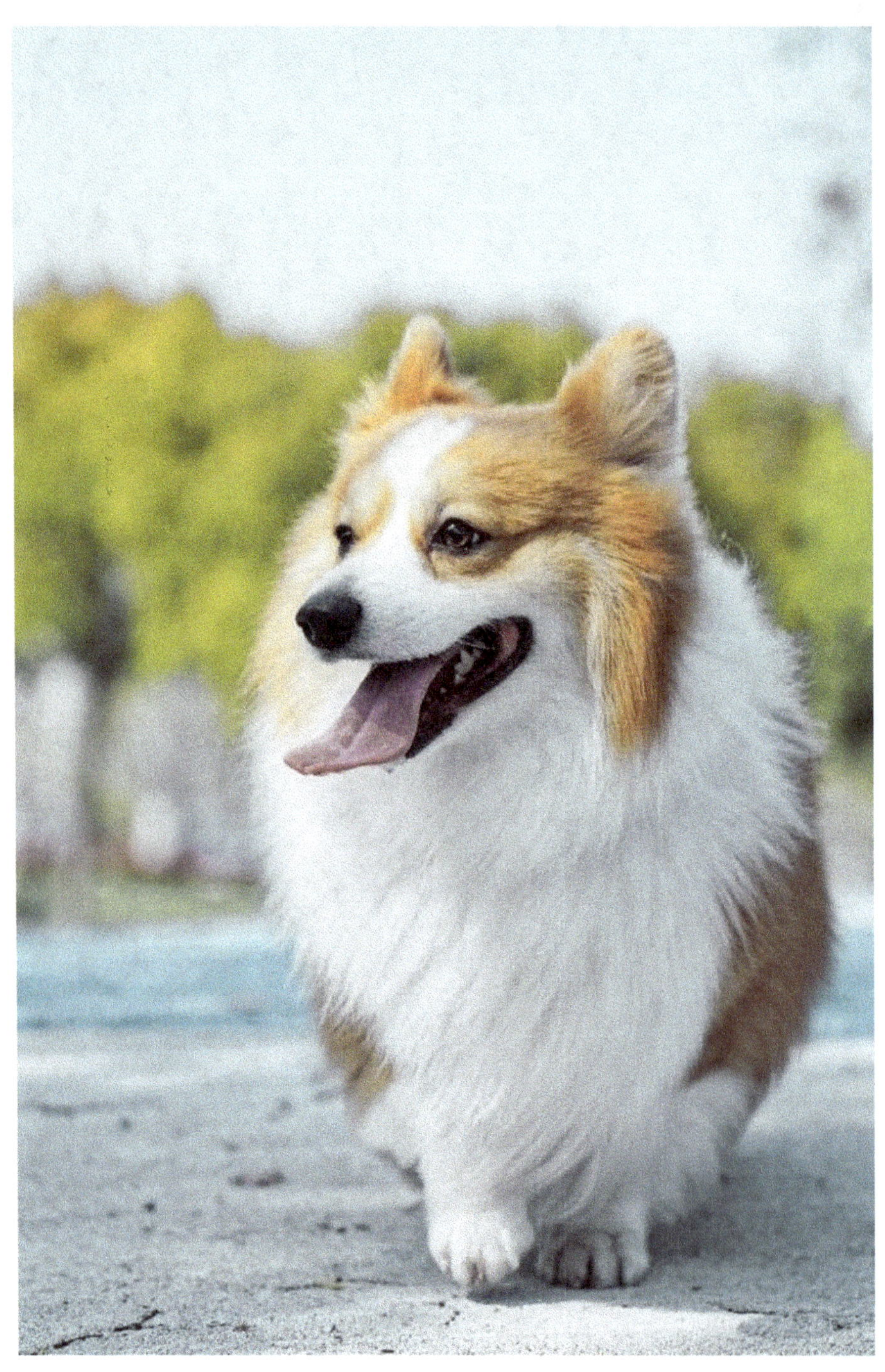

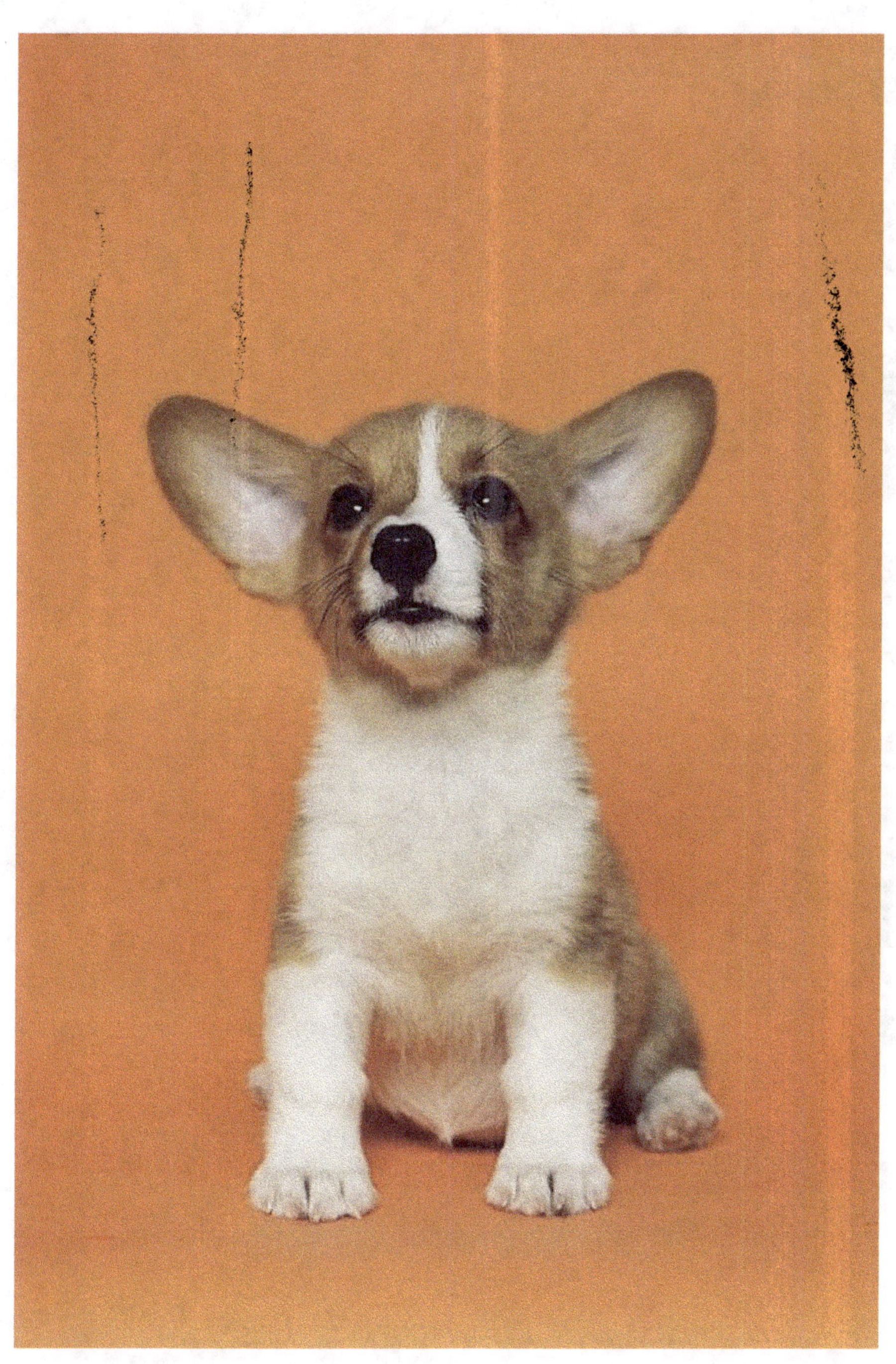

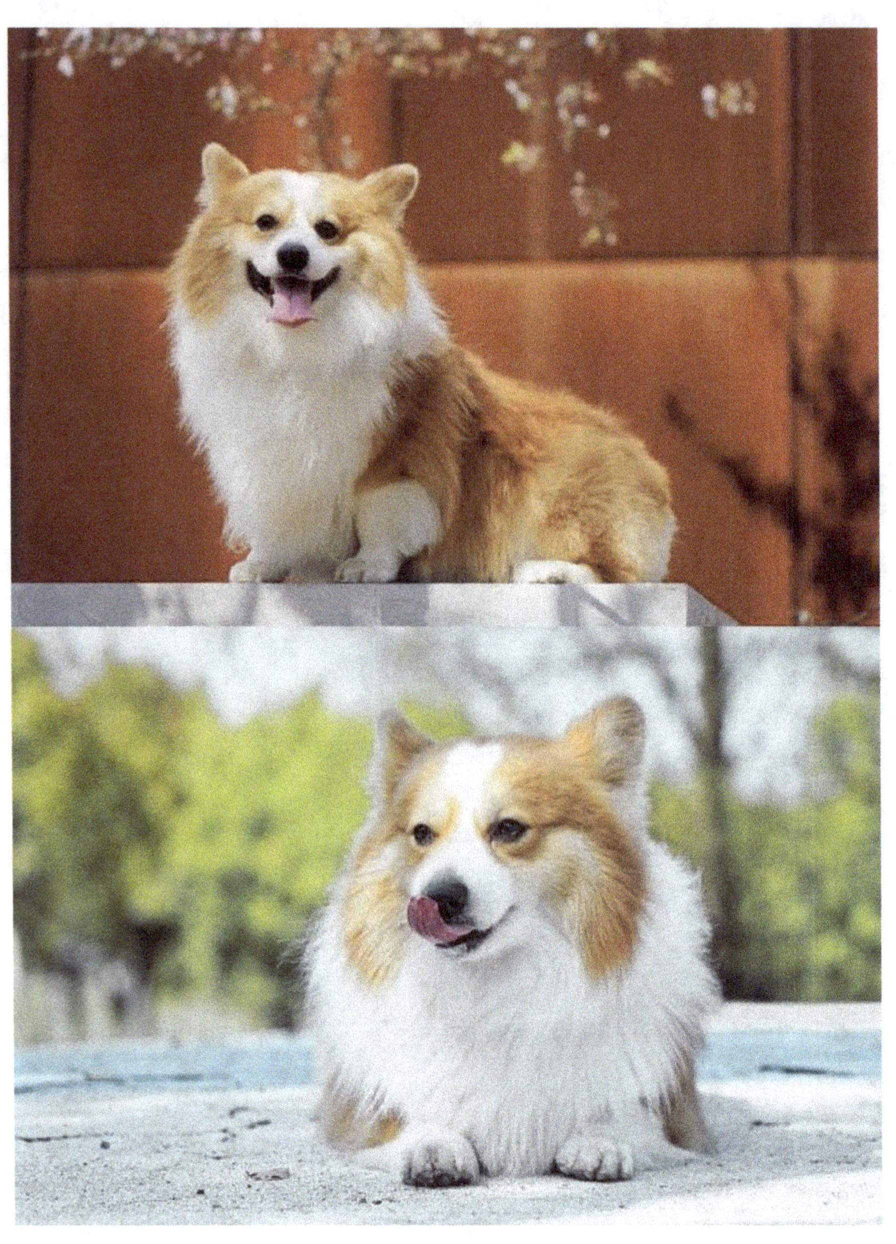

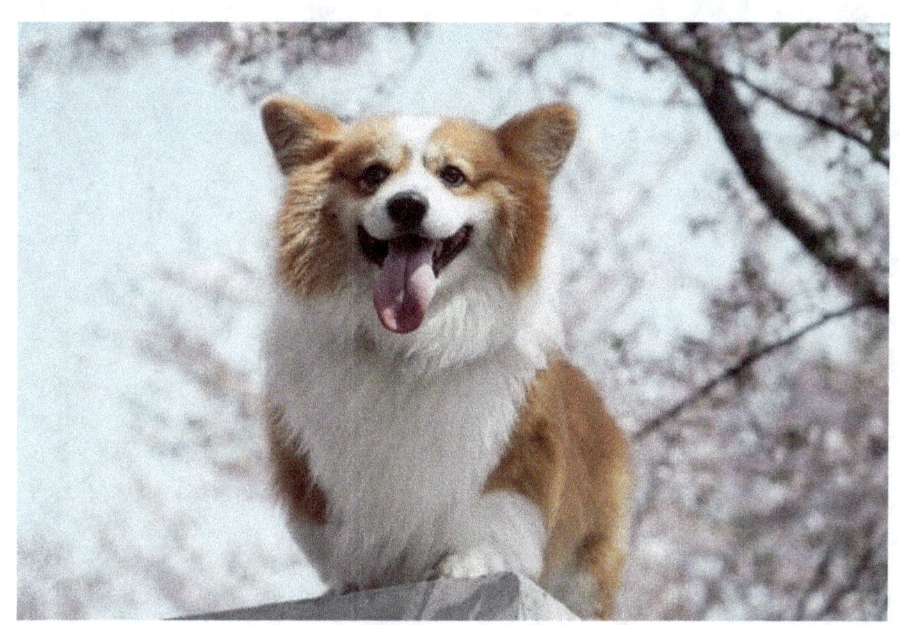

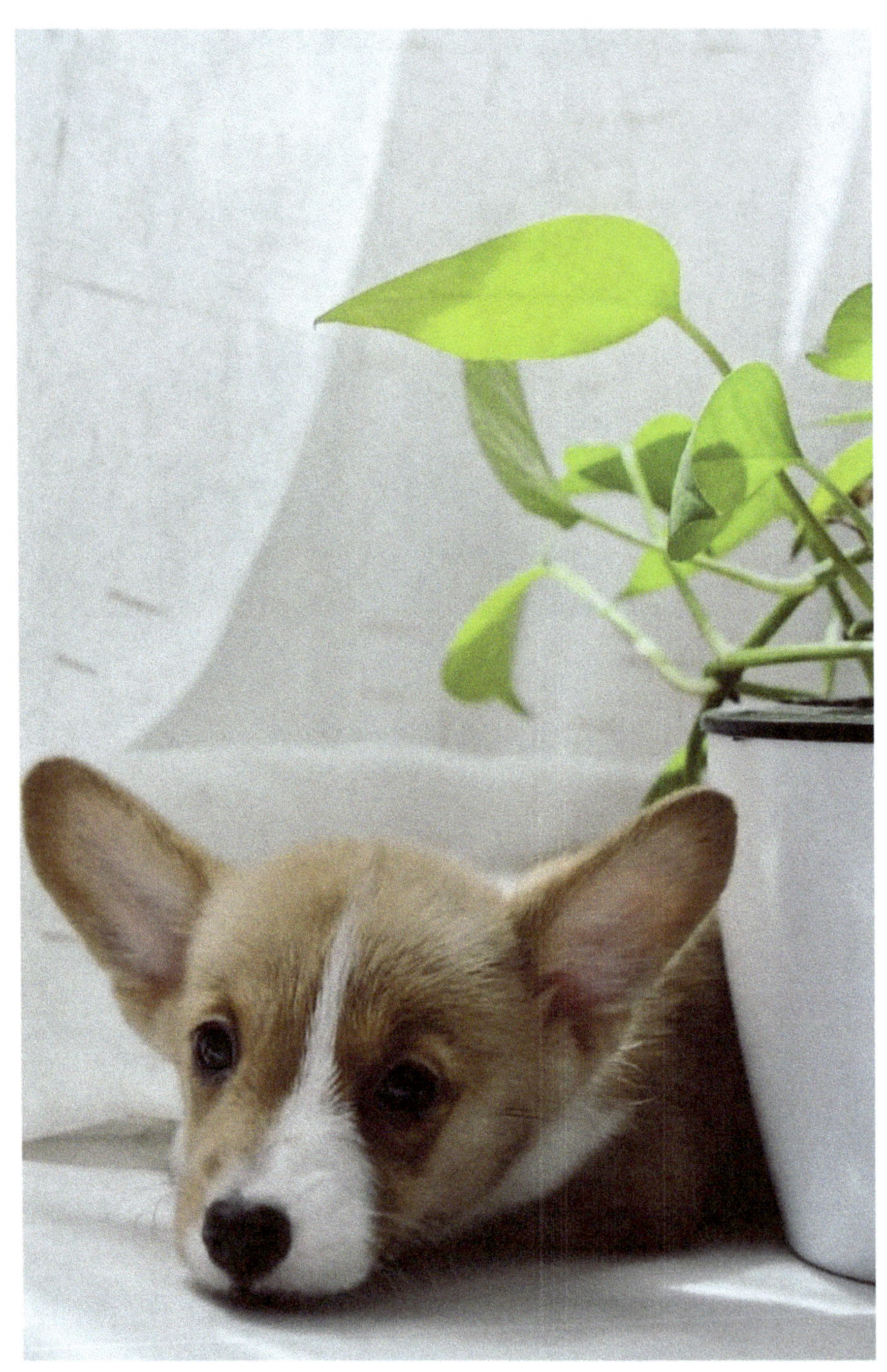

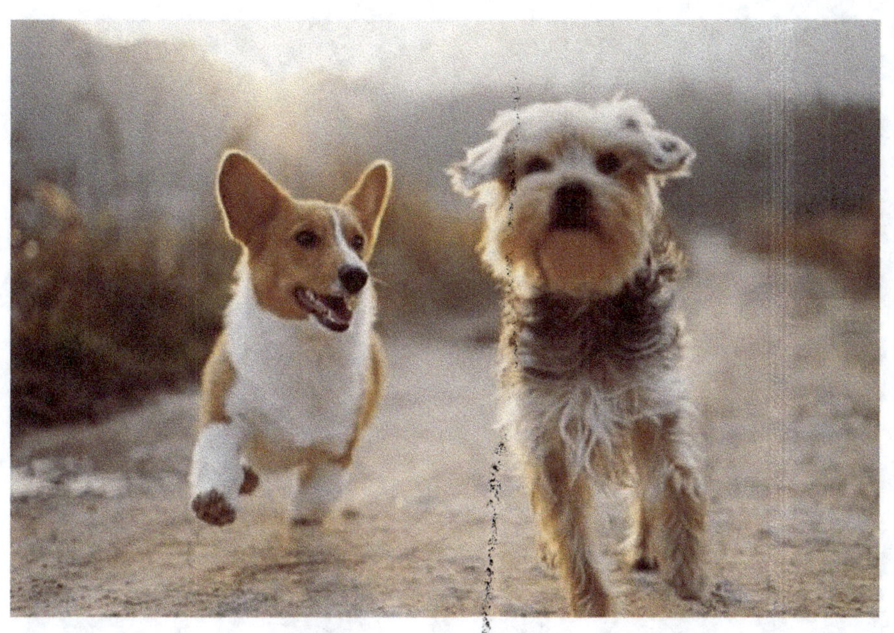

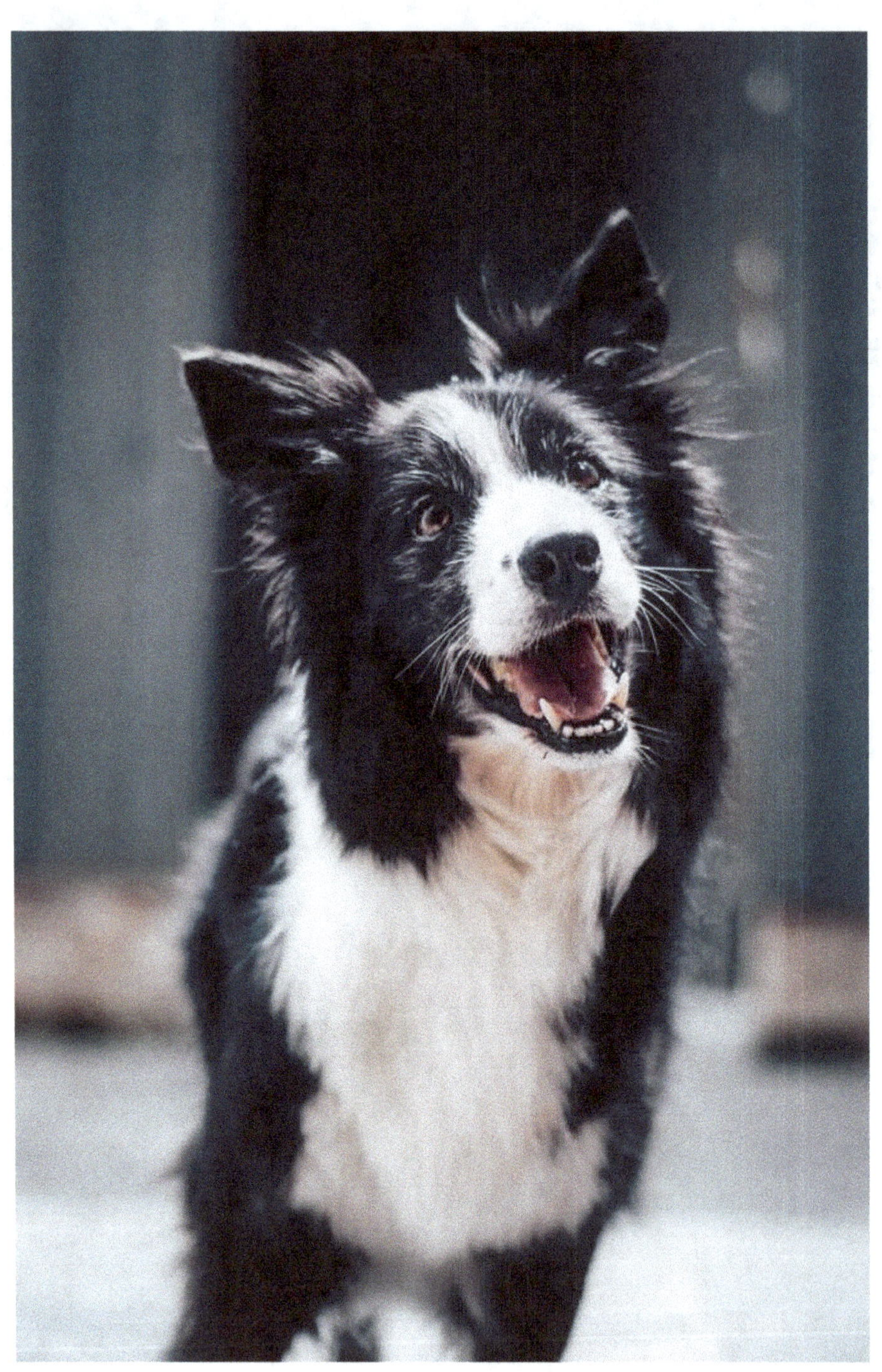

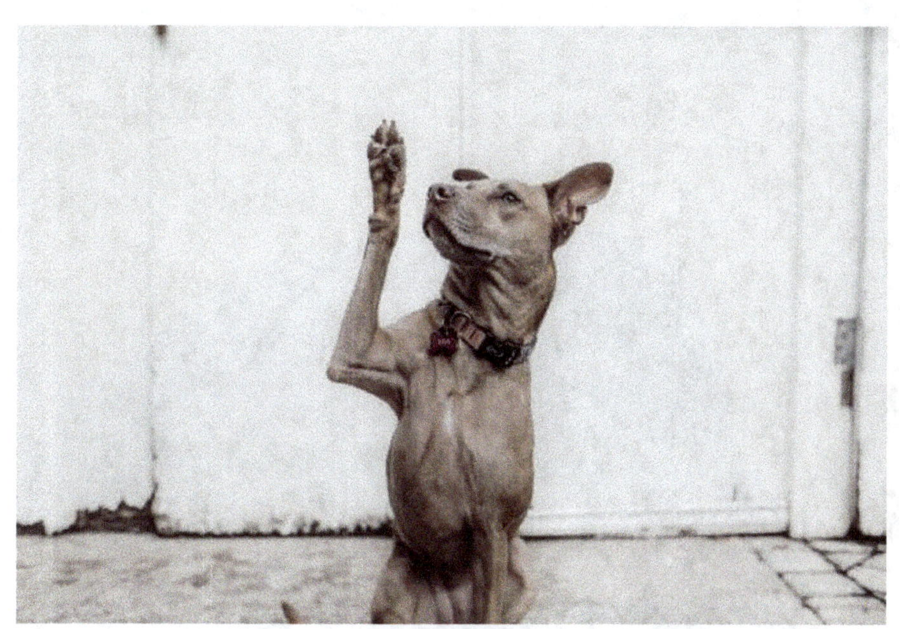

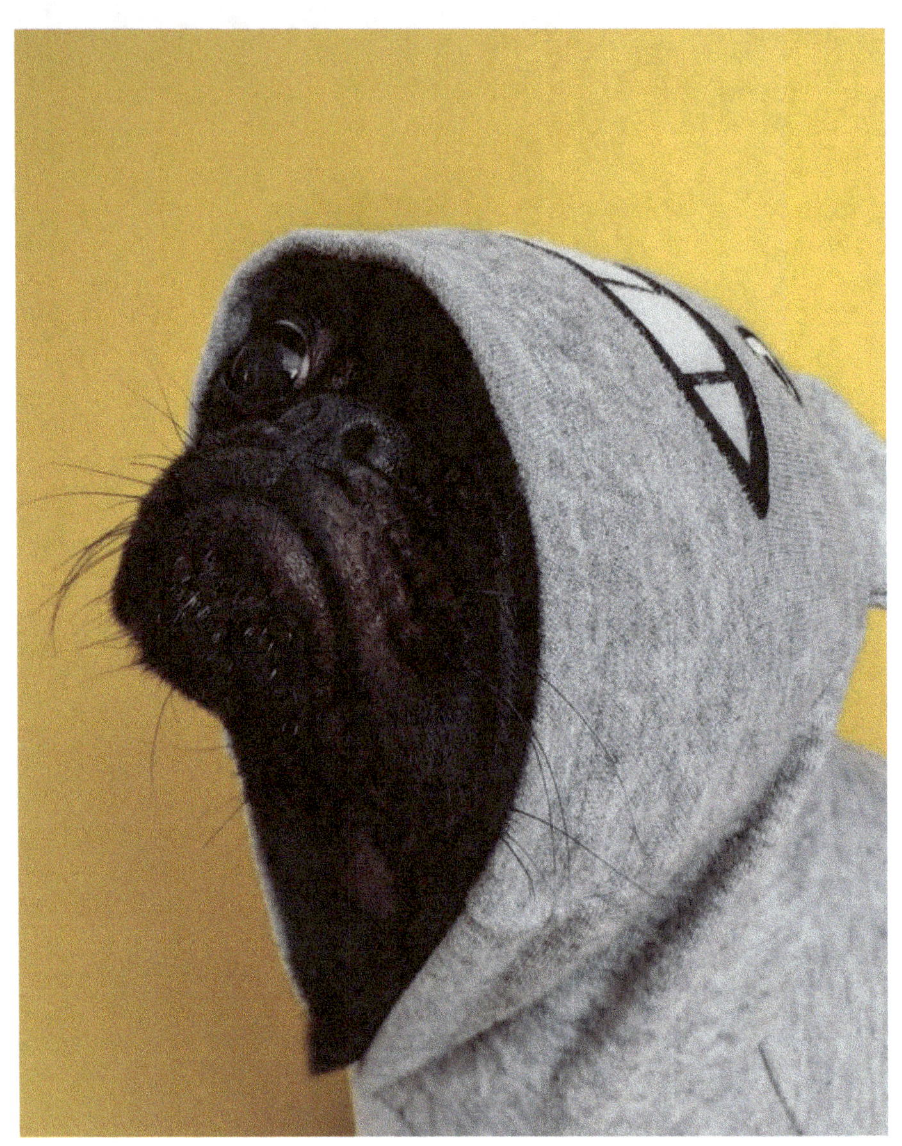

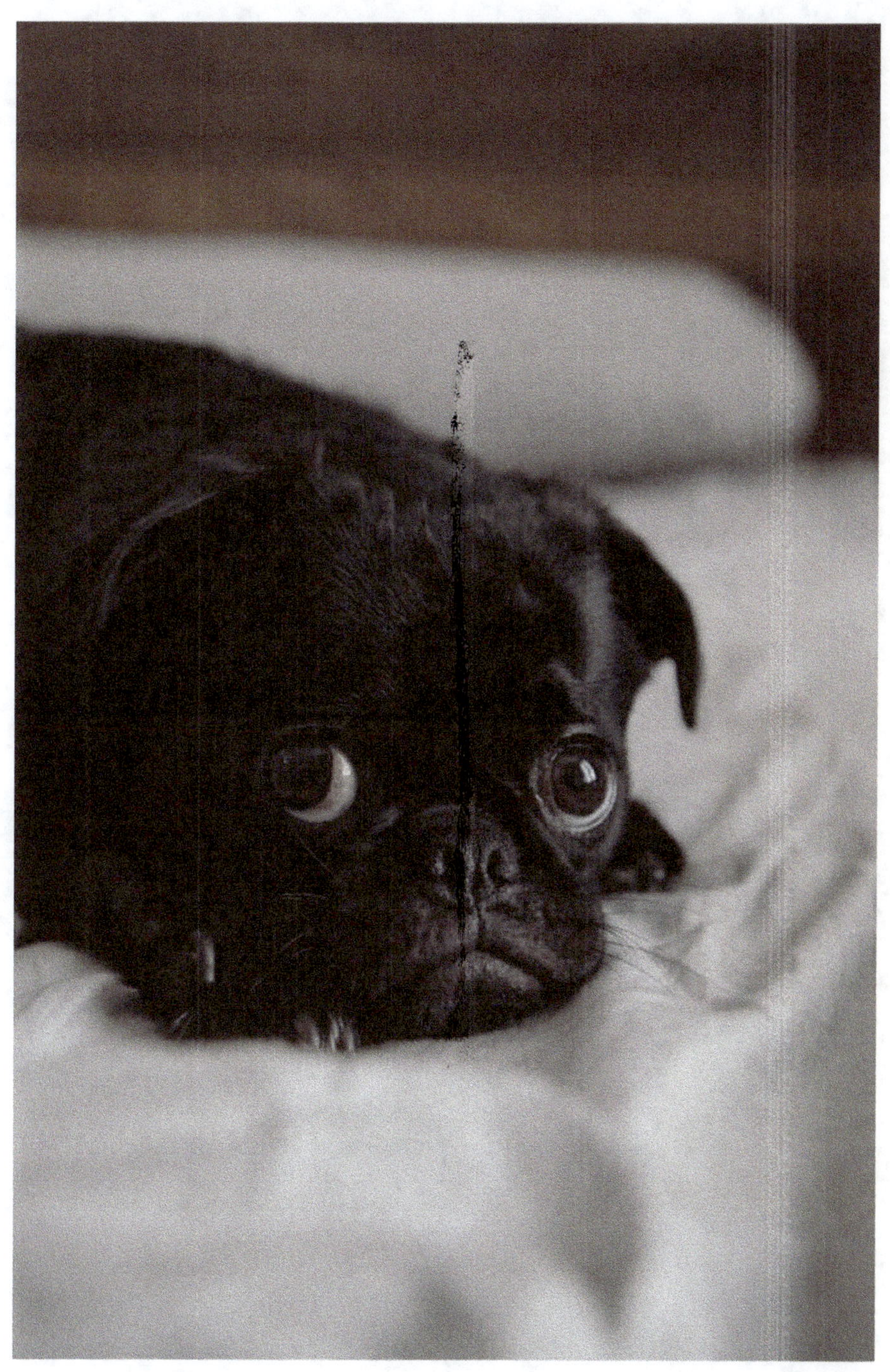

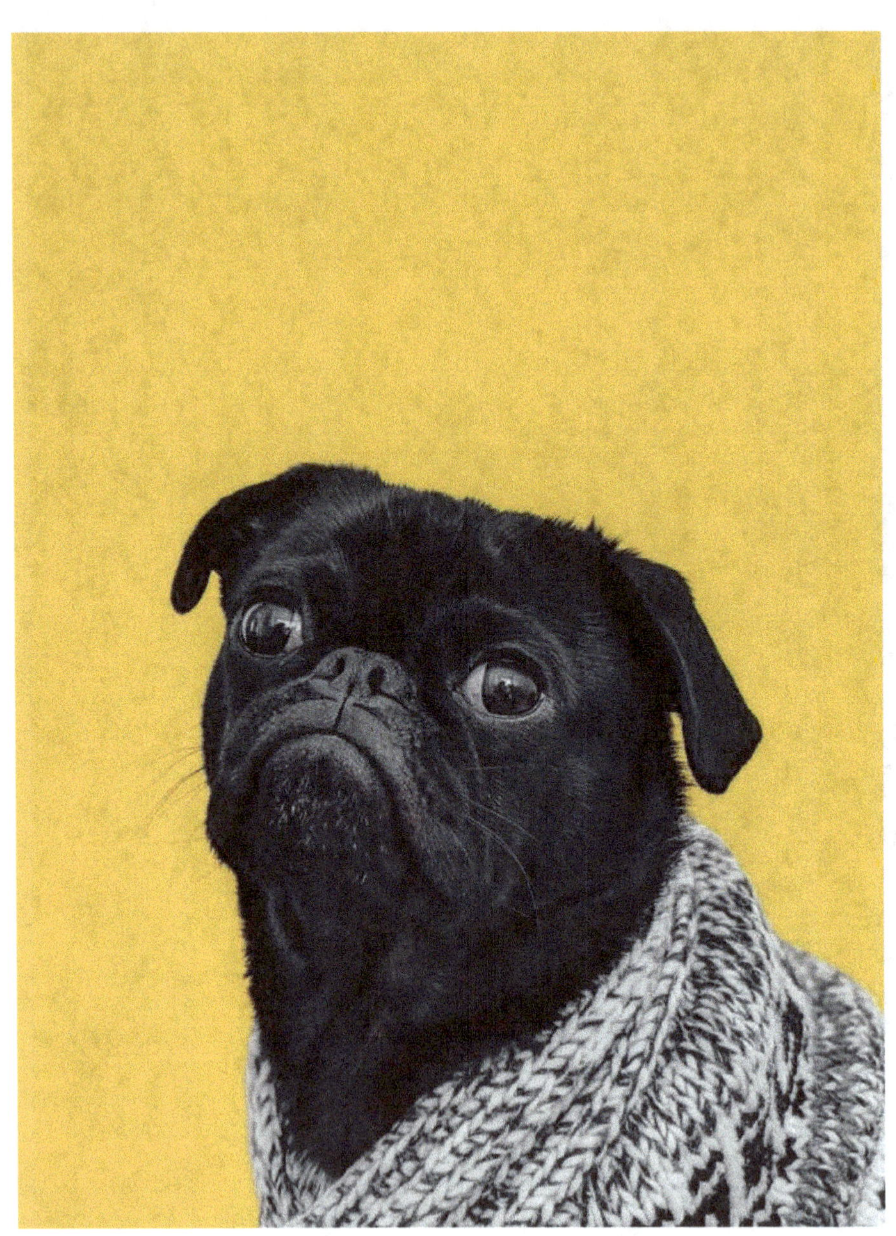

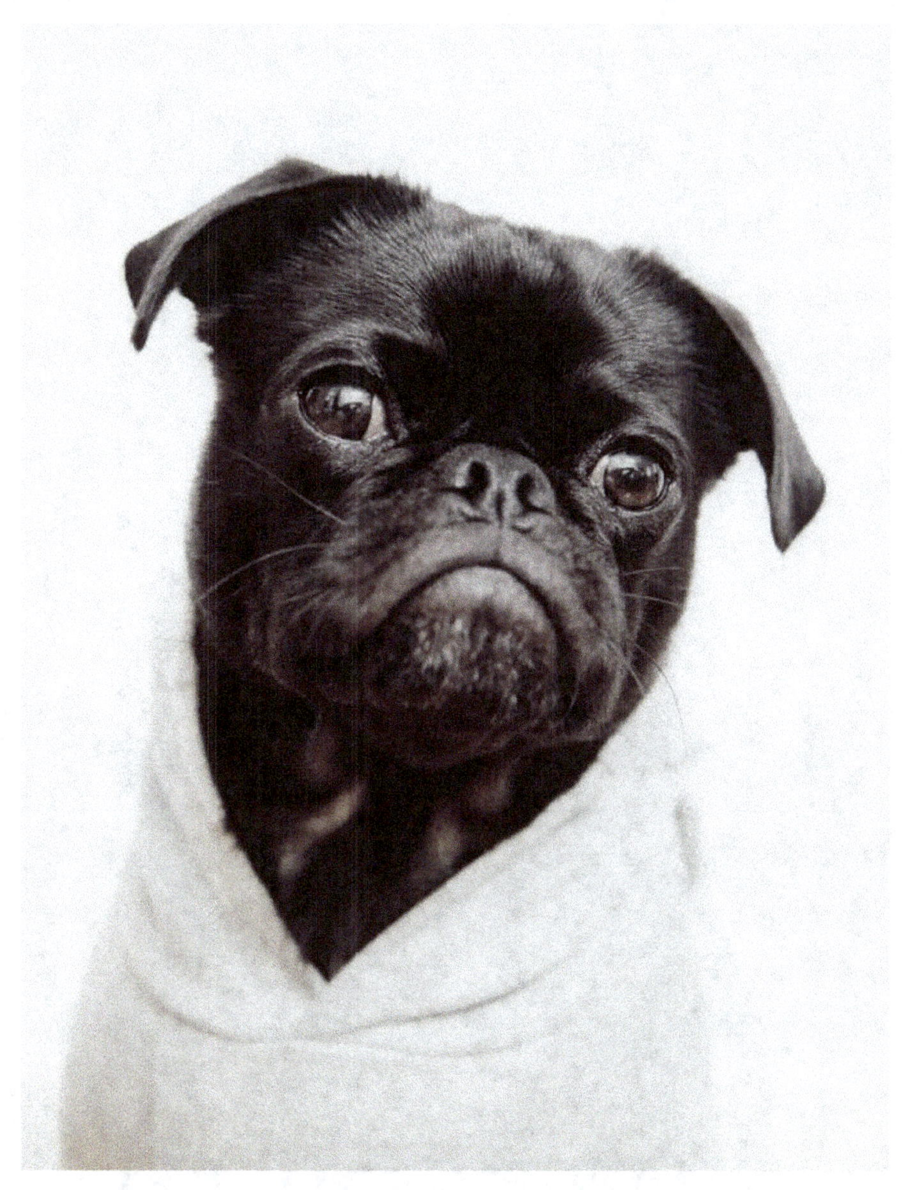

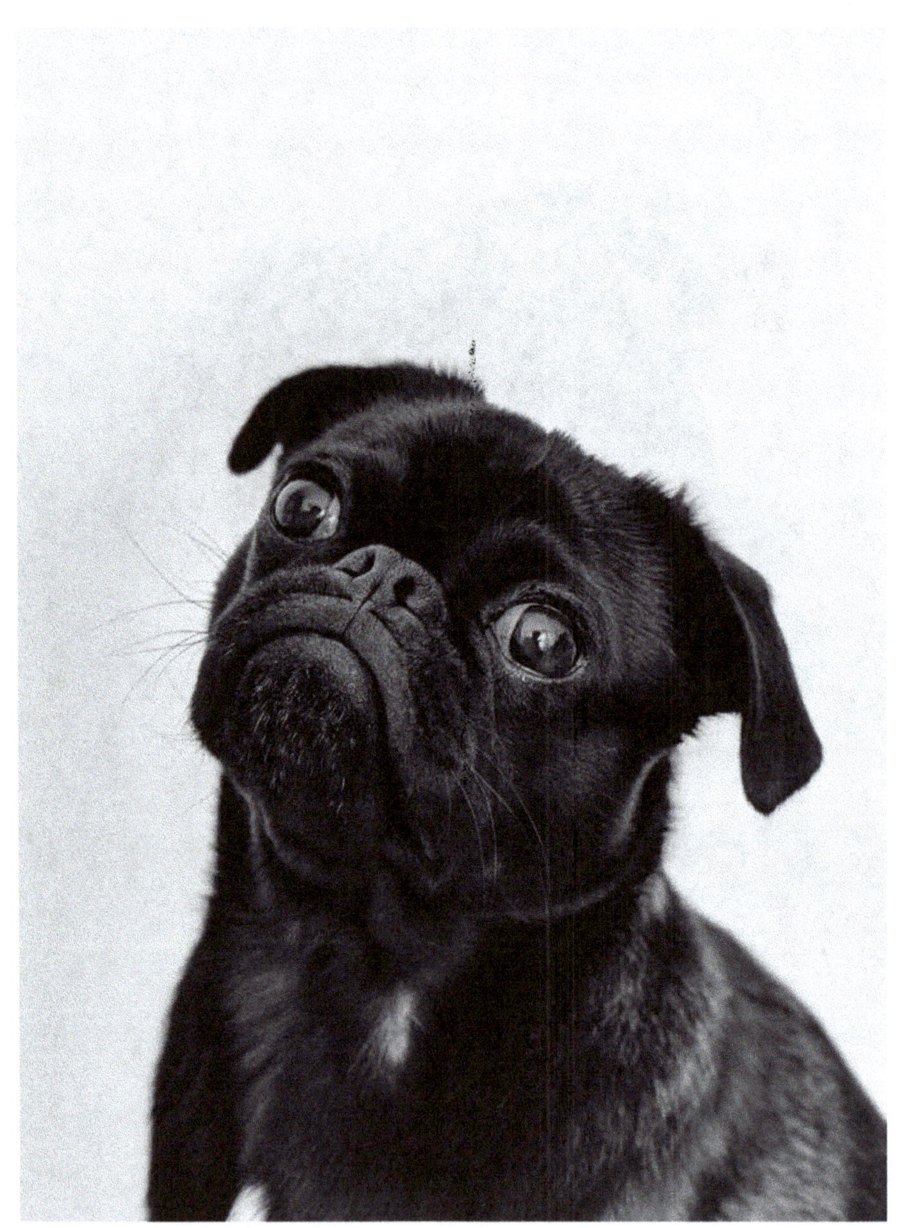

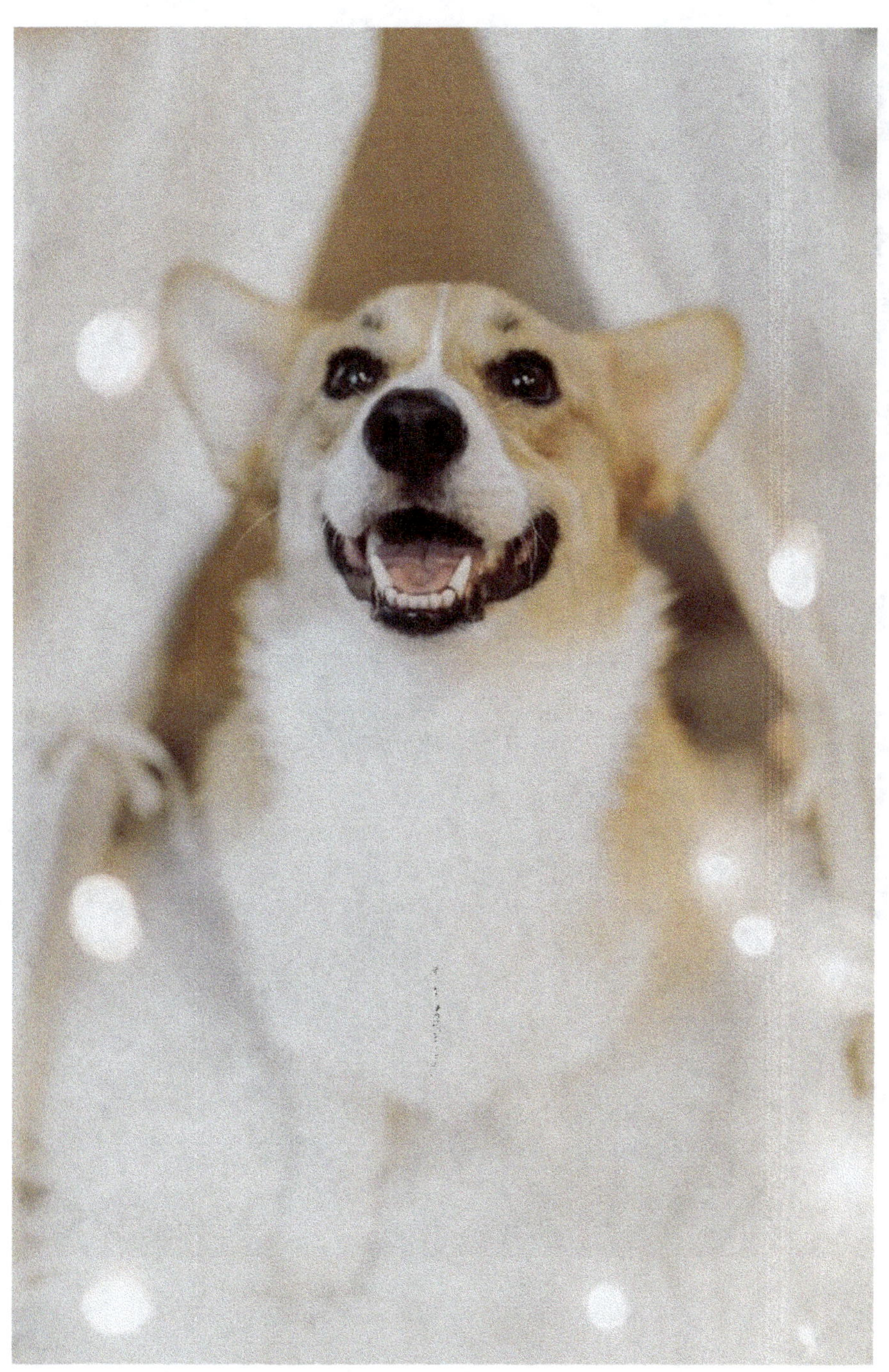

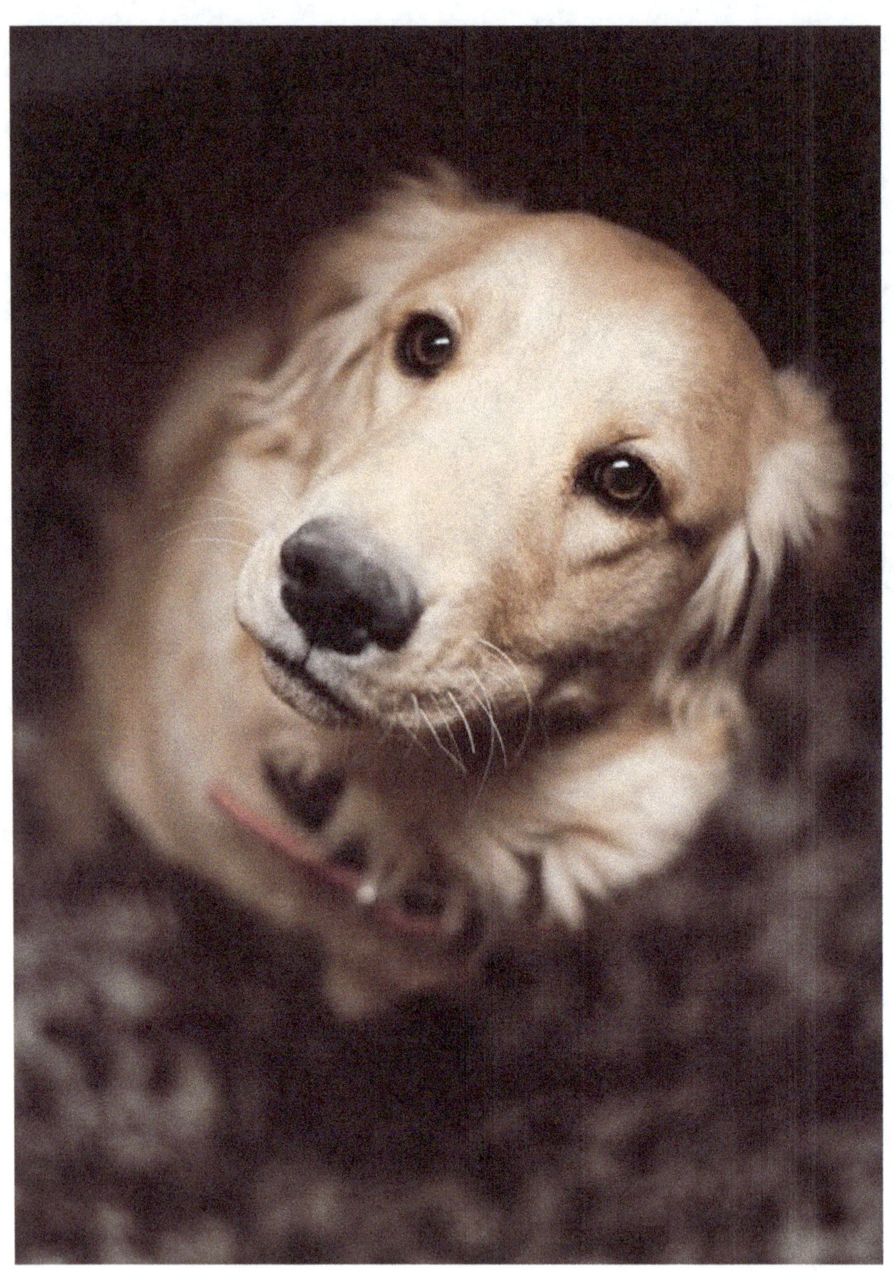

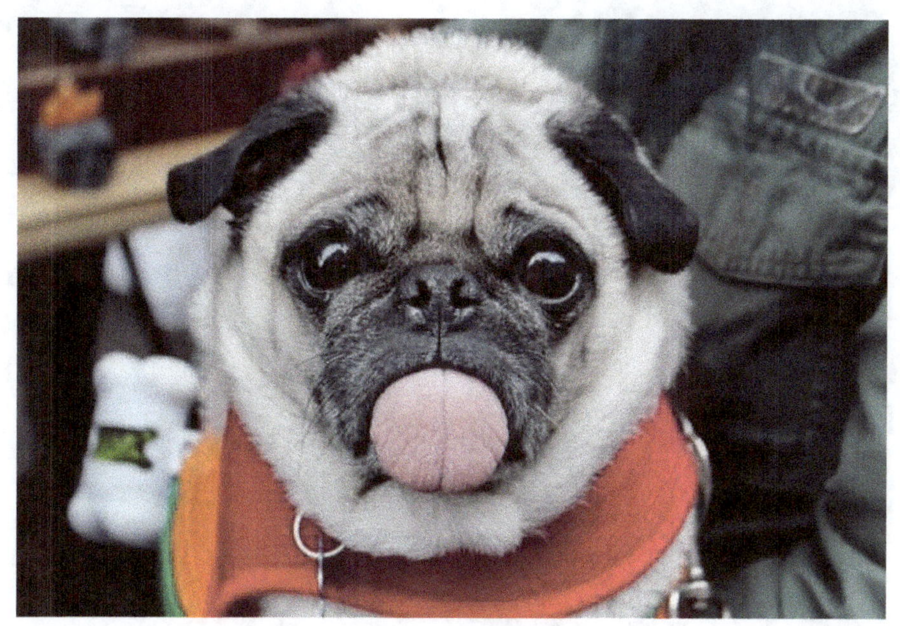

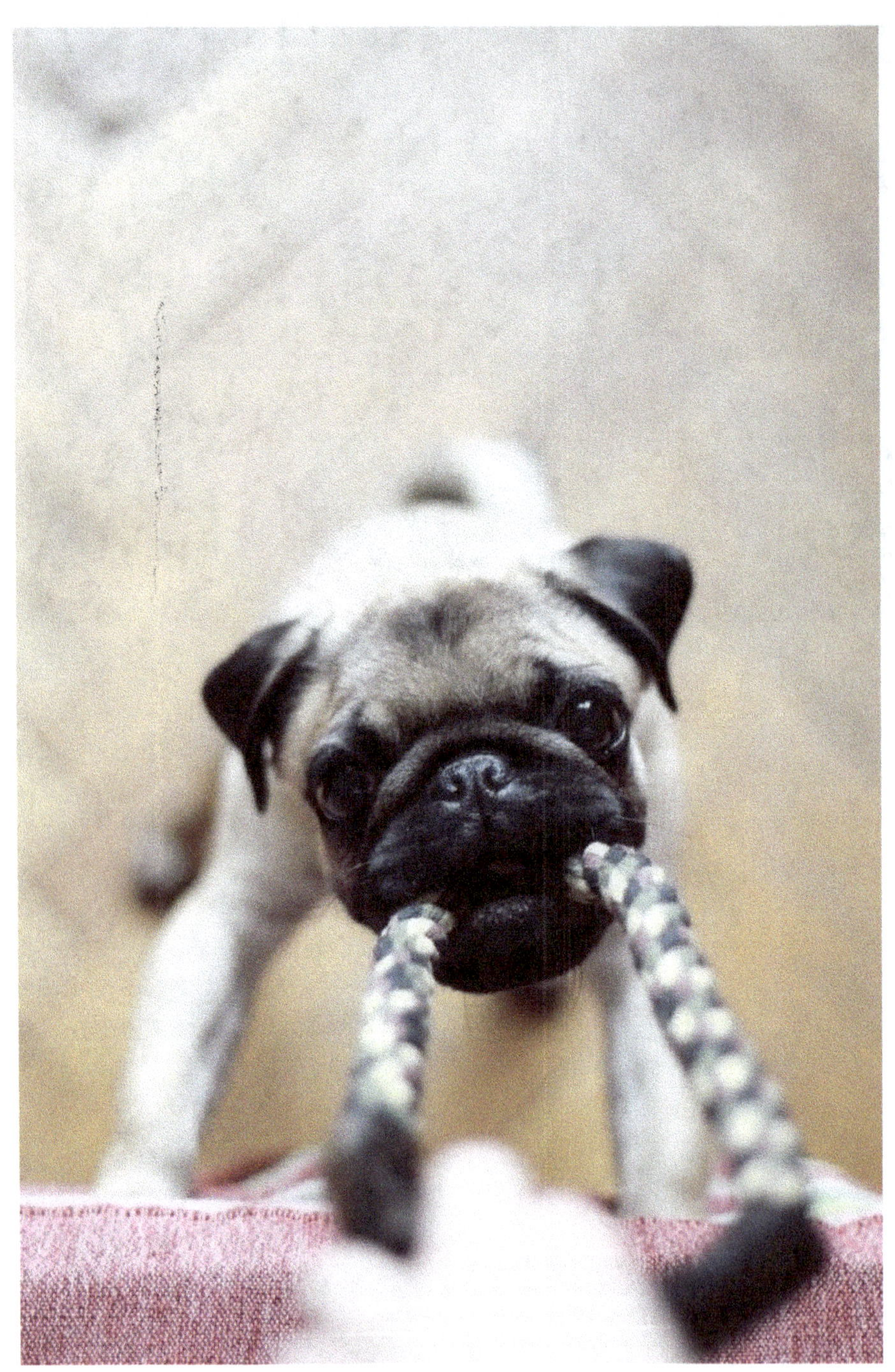

26

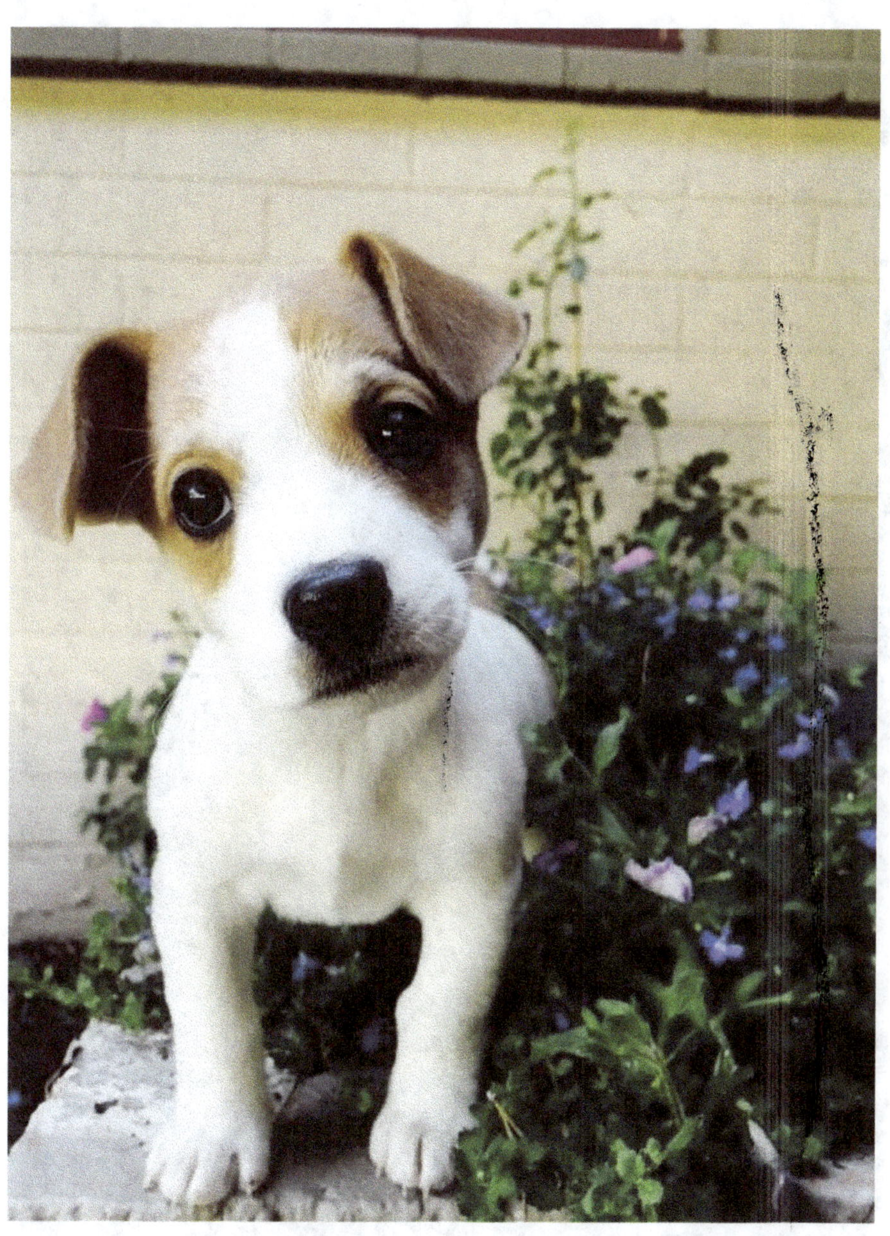

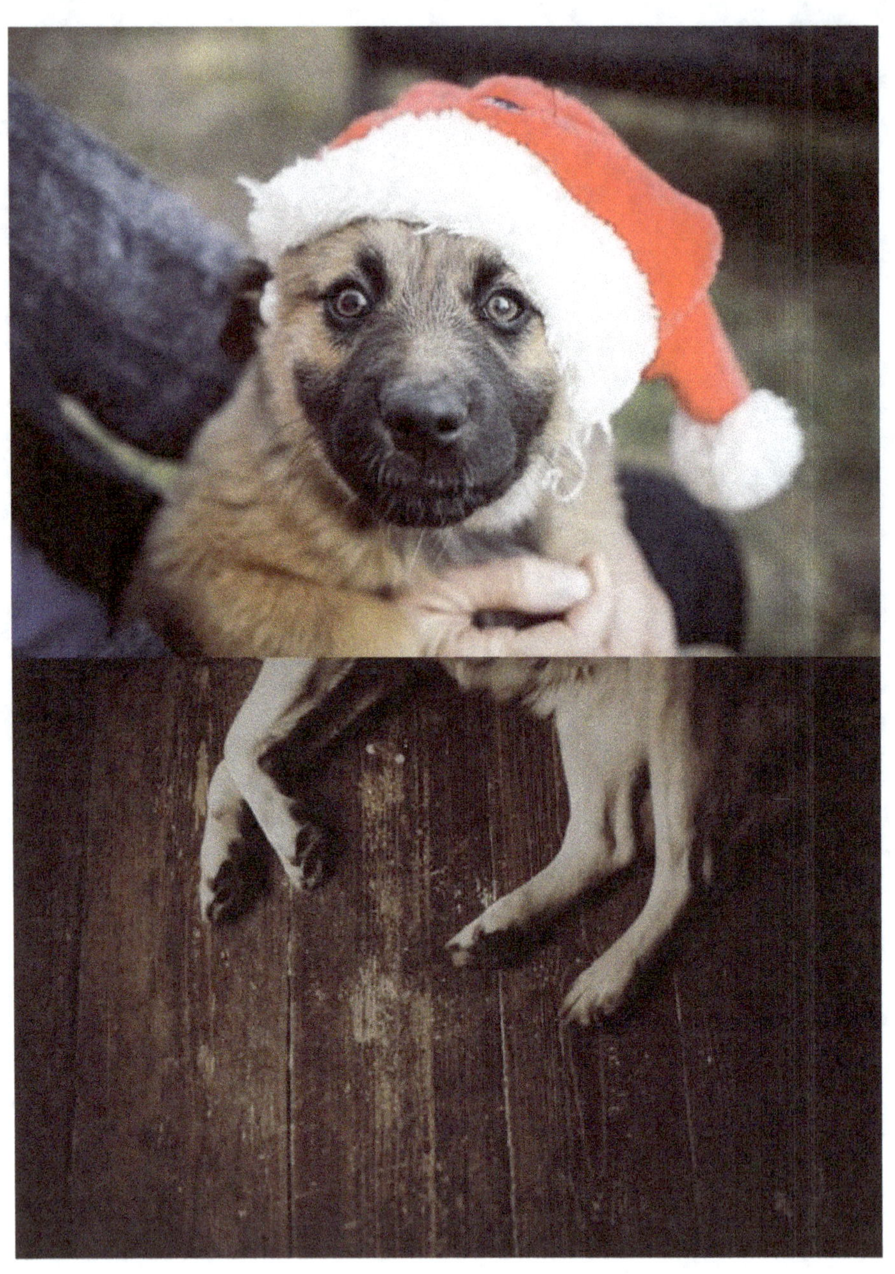

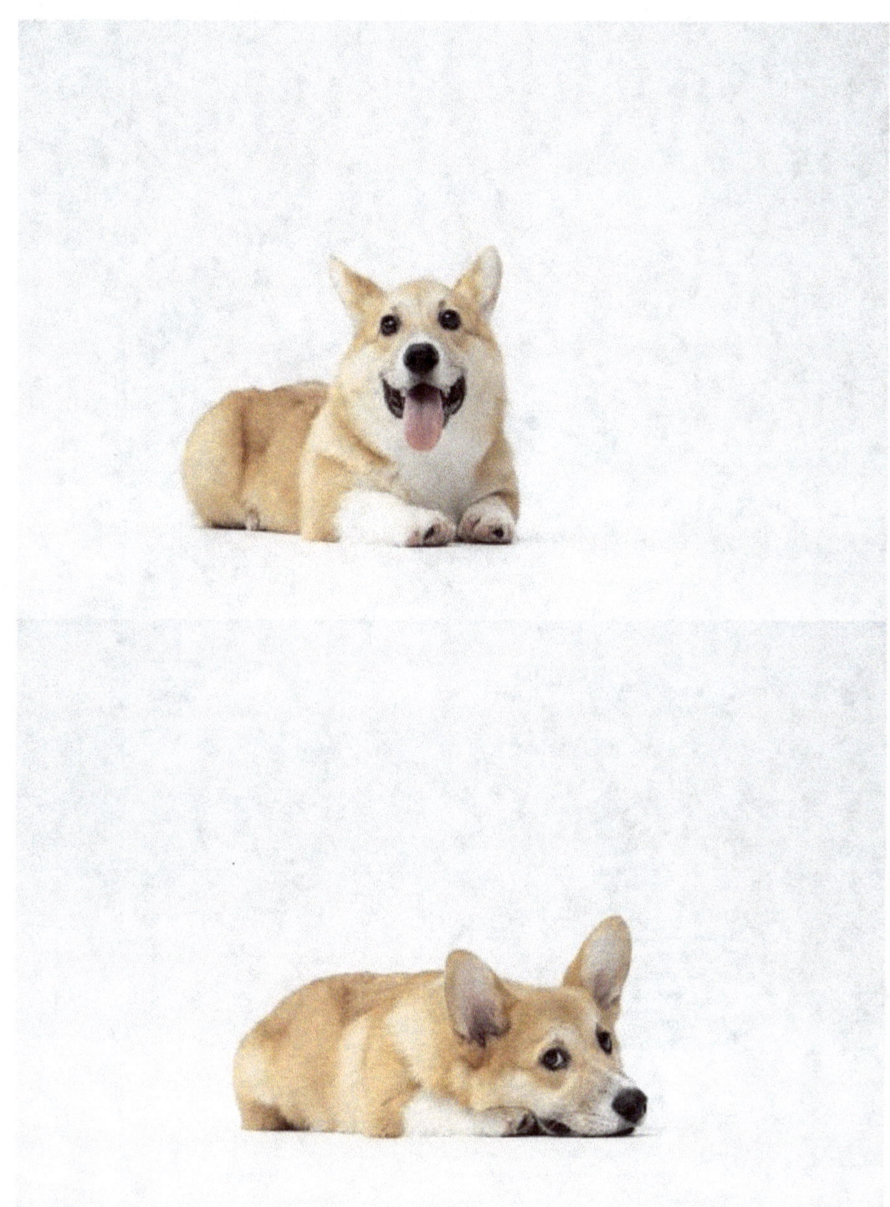

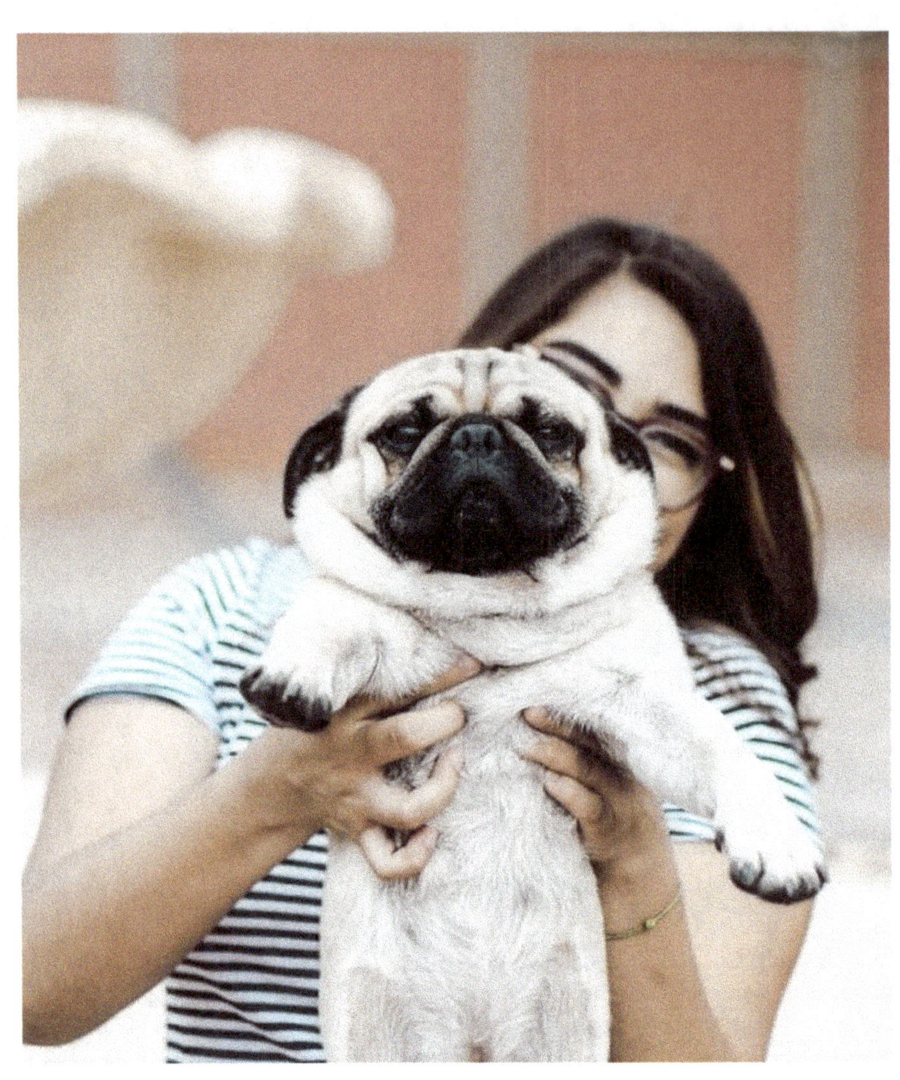

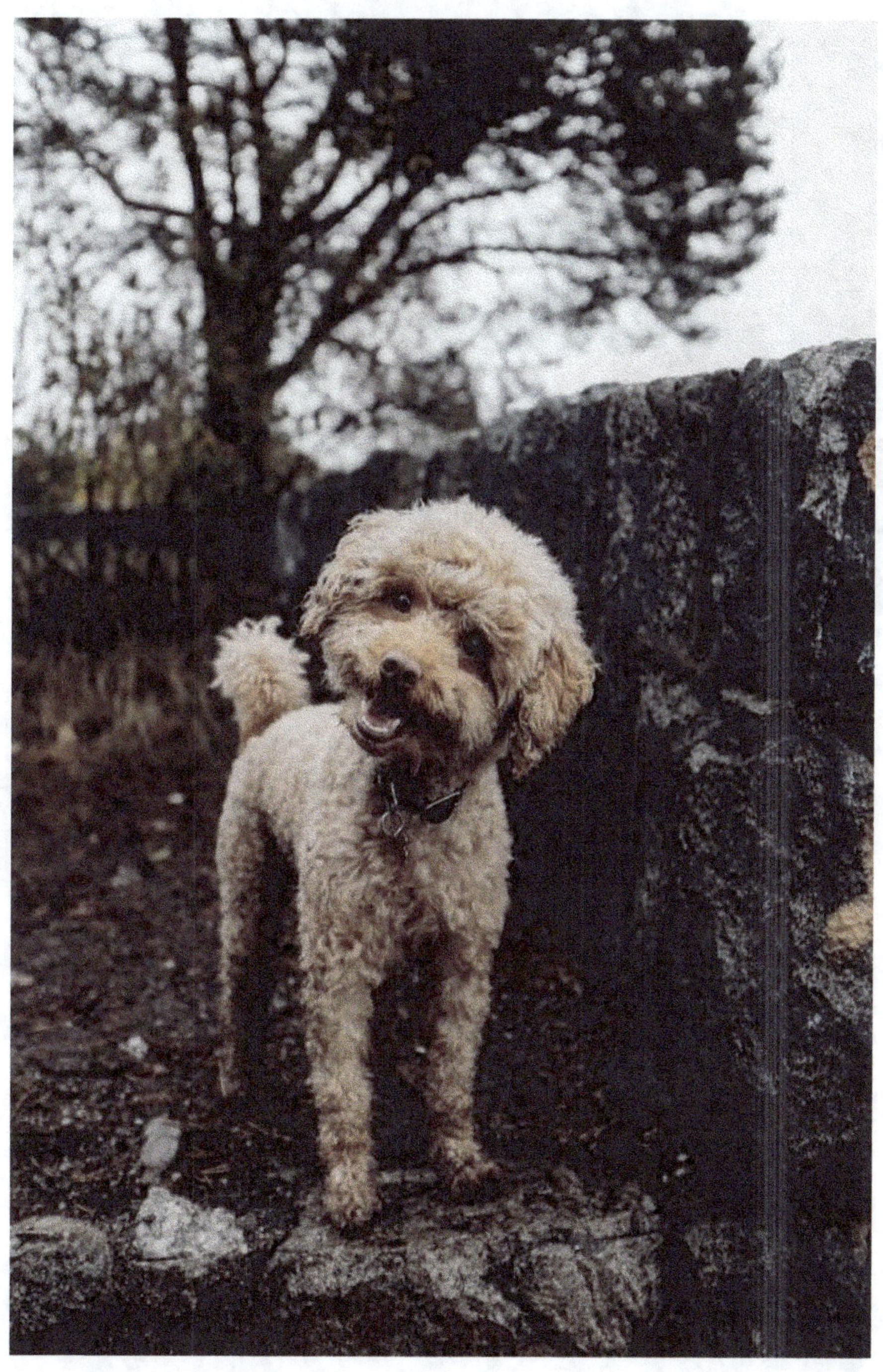

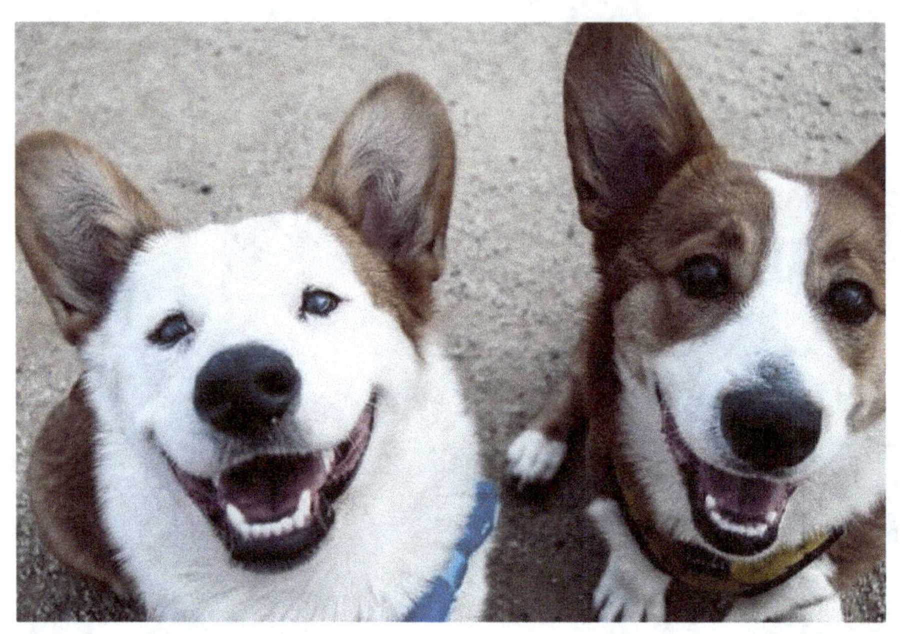

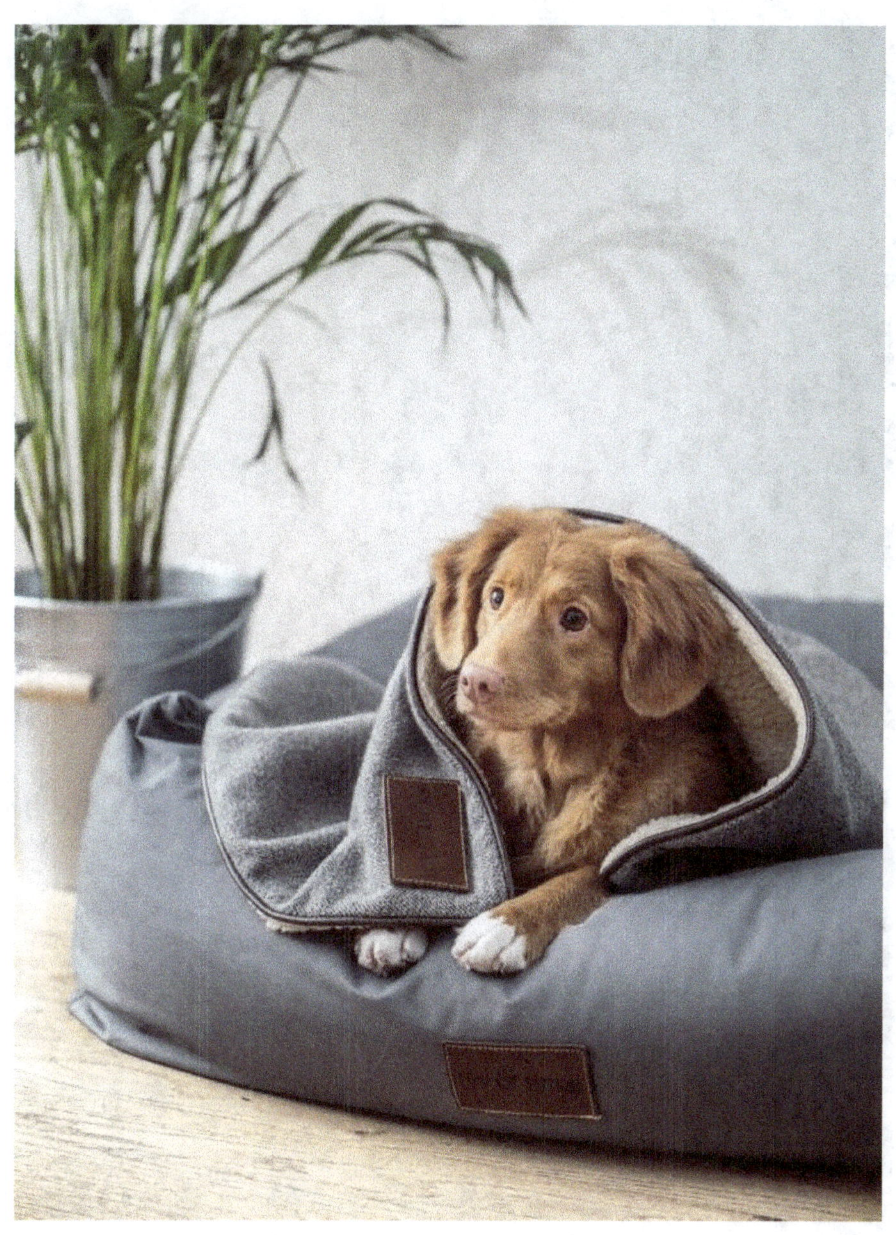

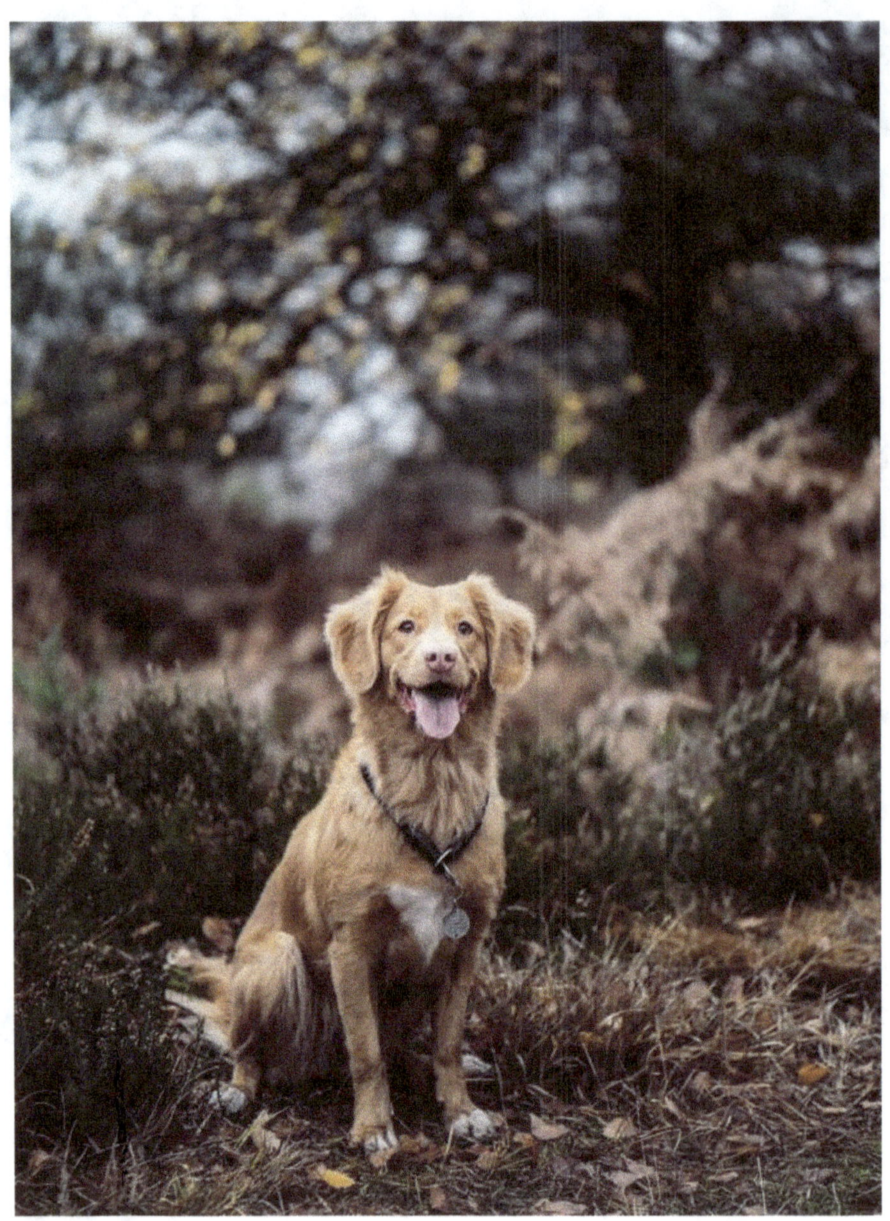

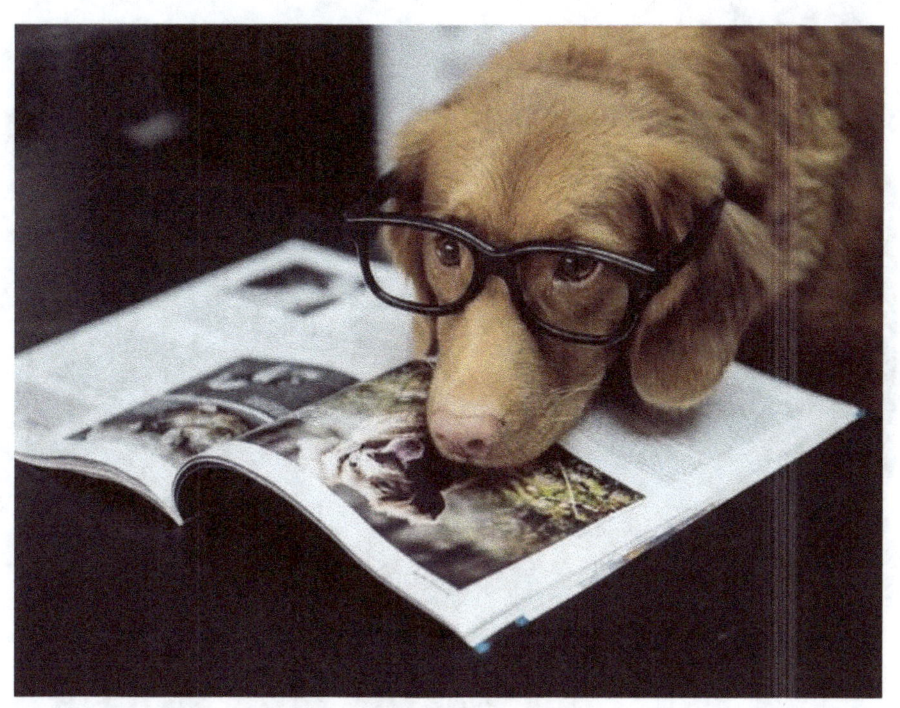

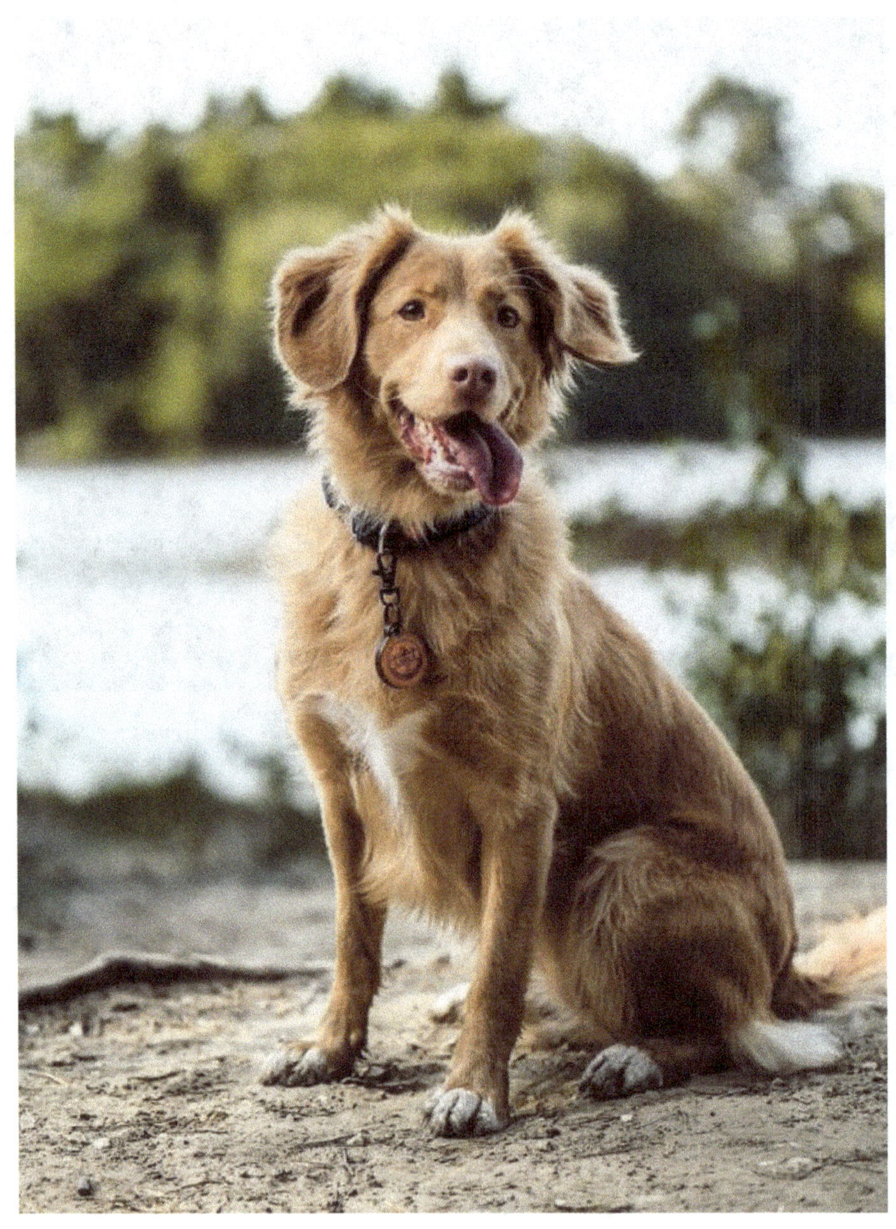

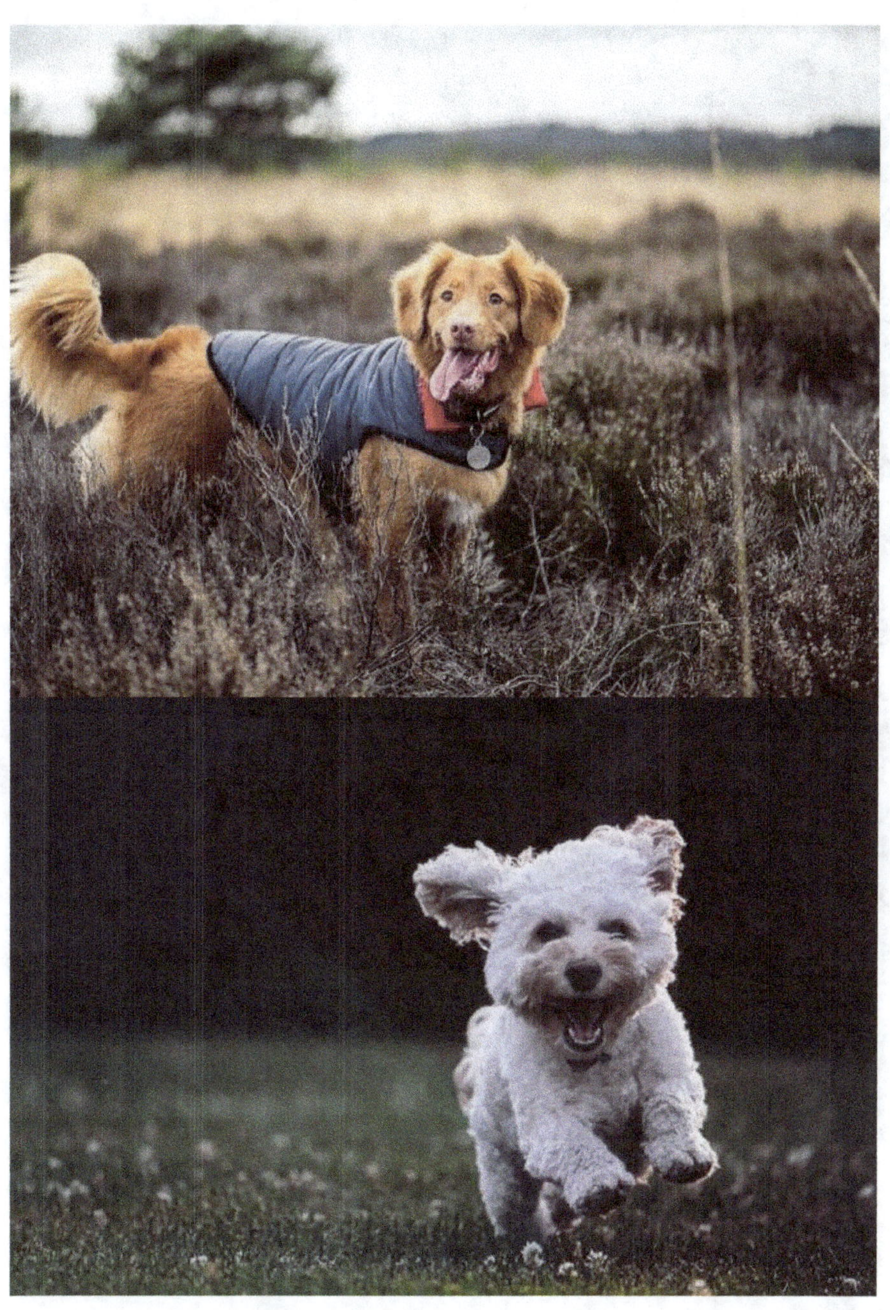

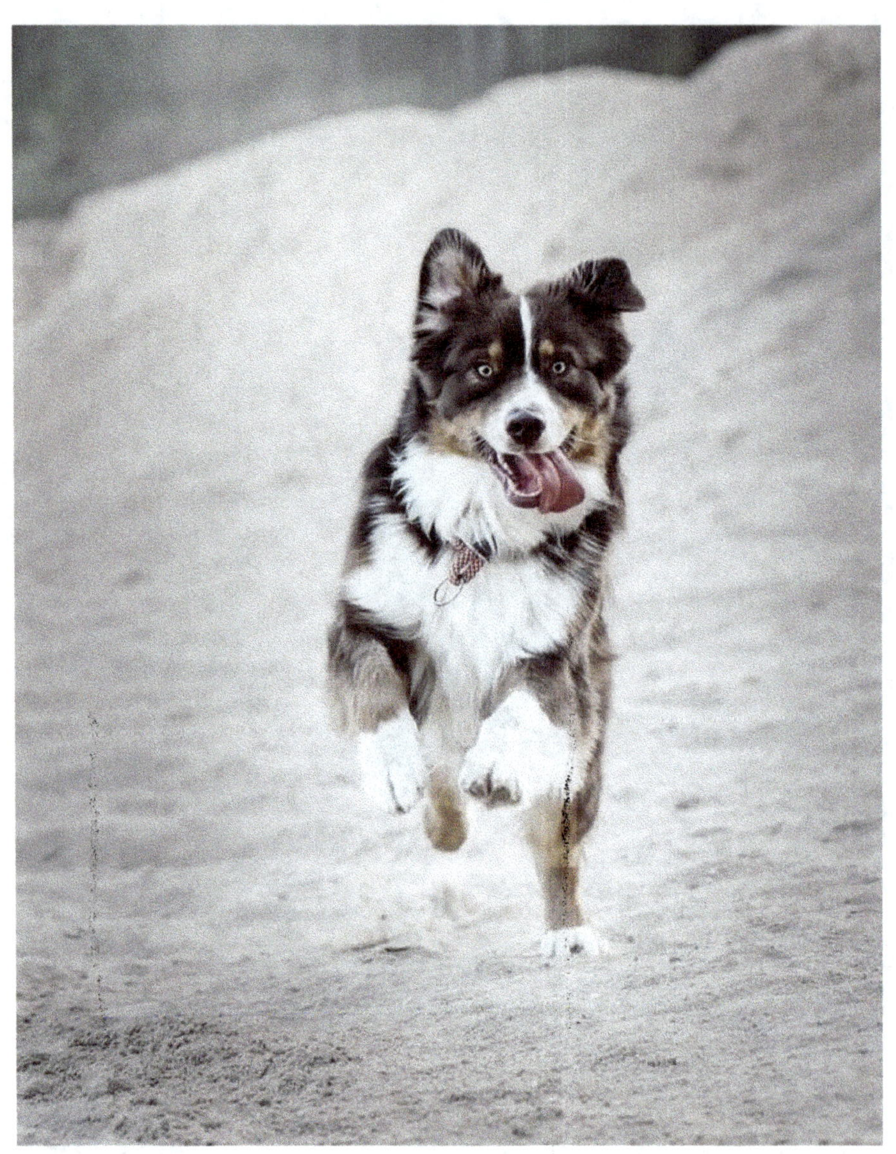

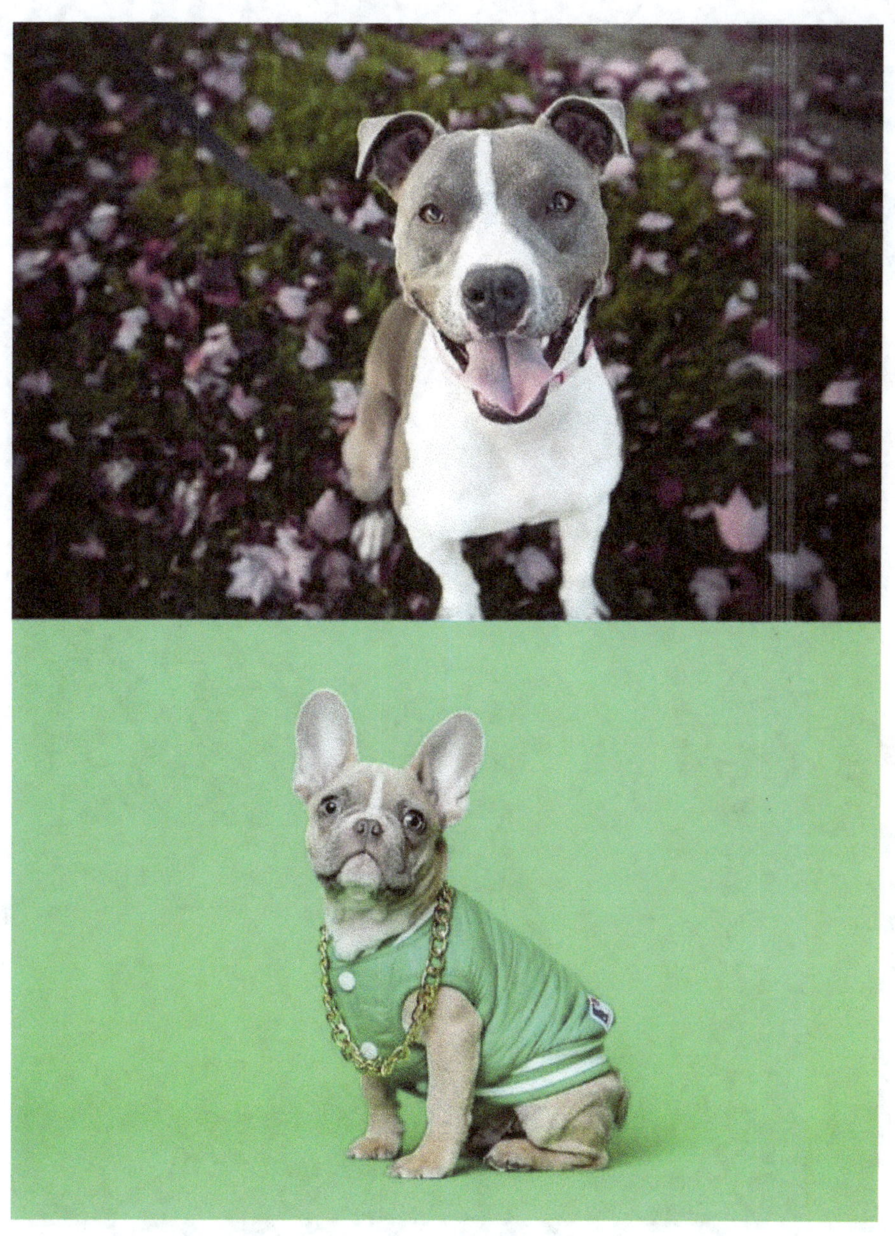

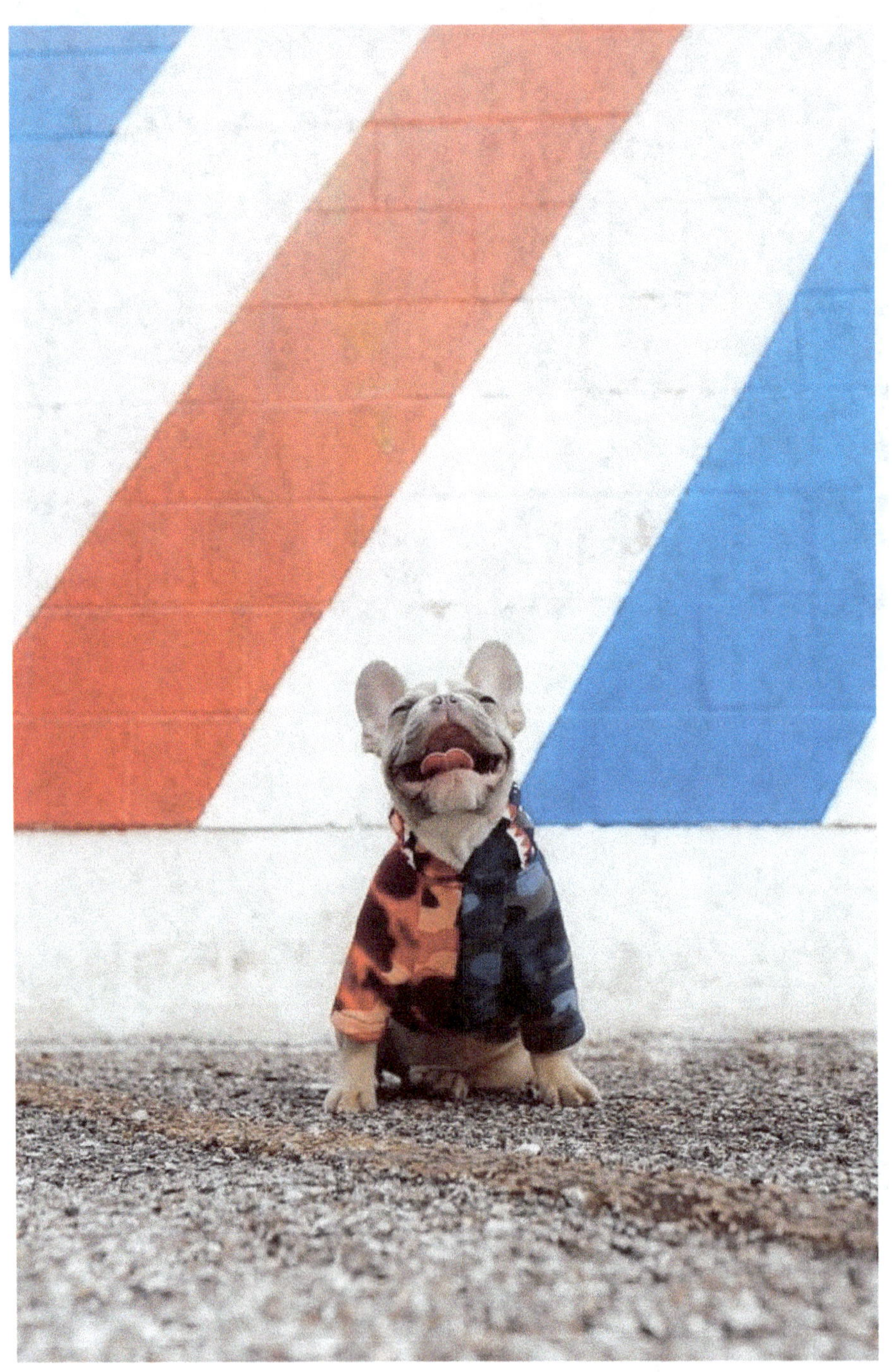

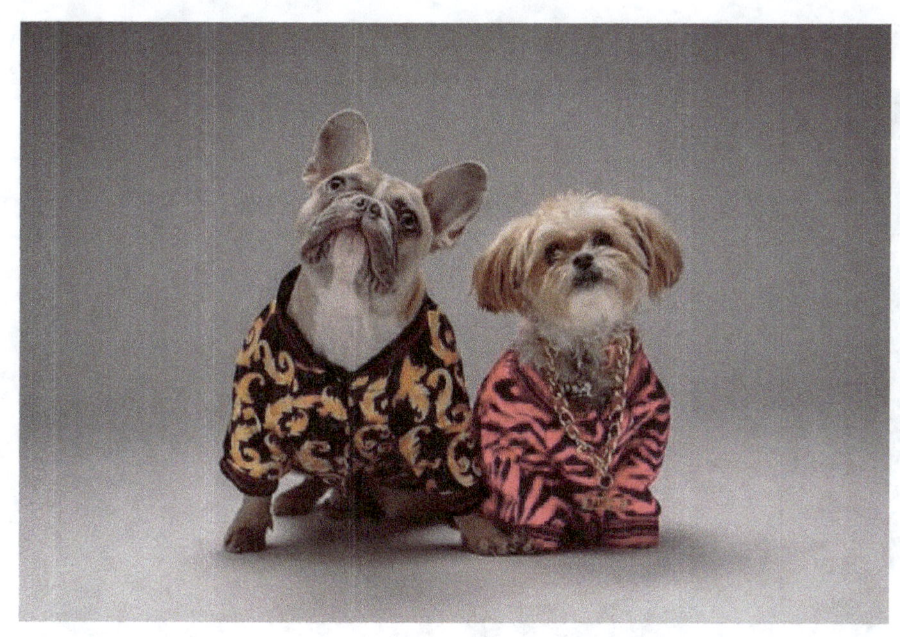

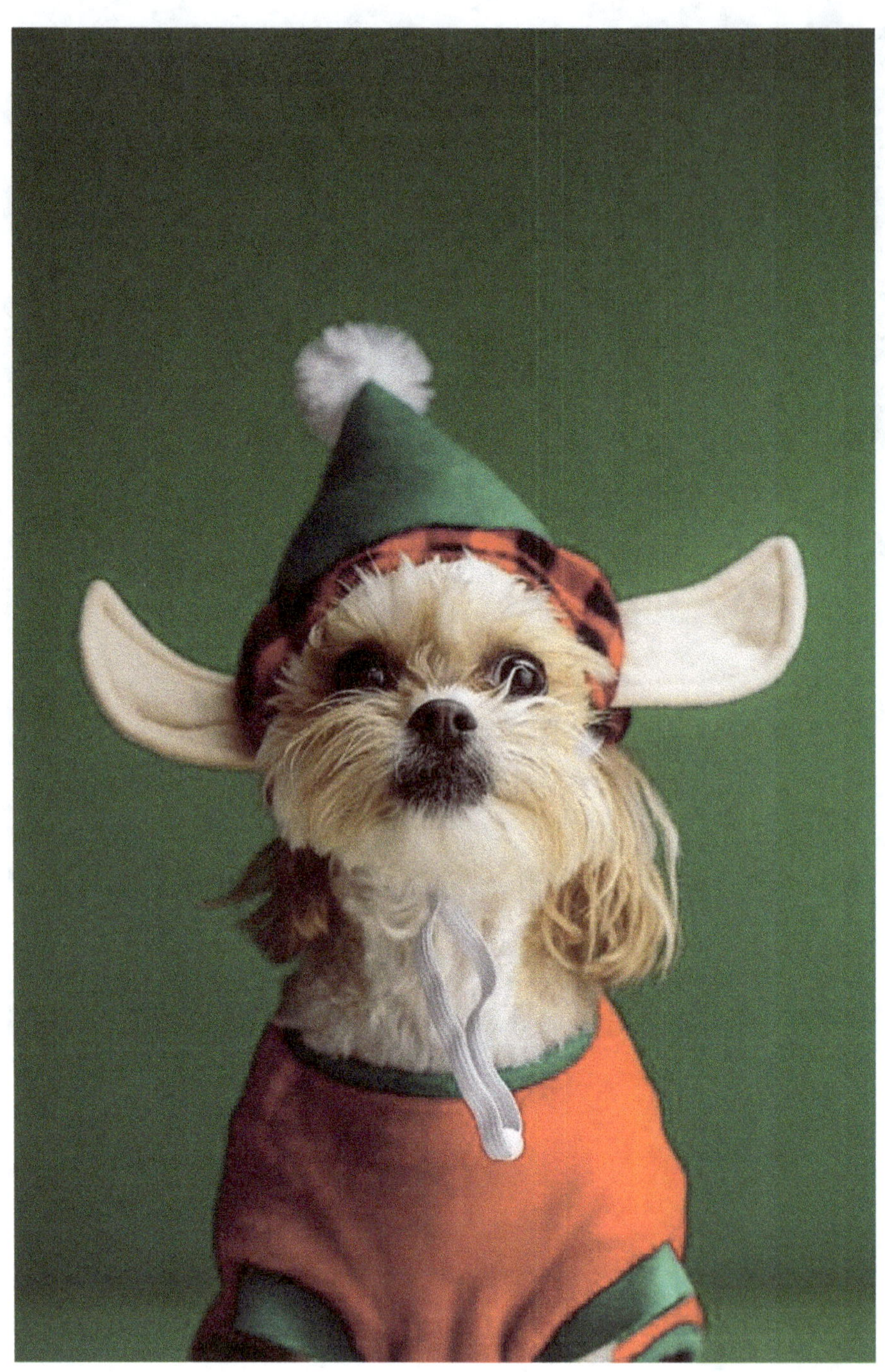

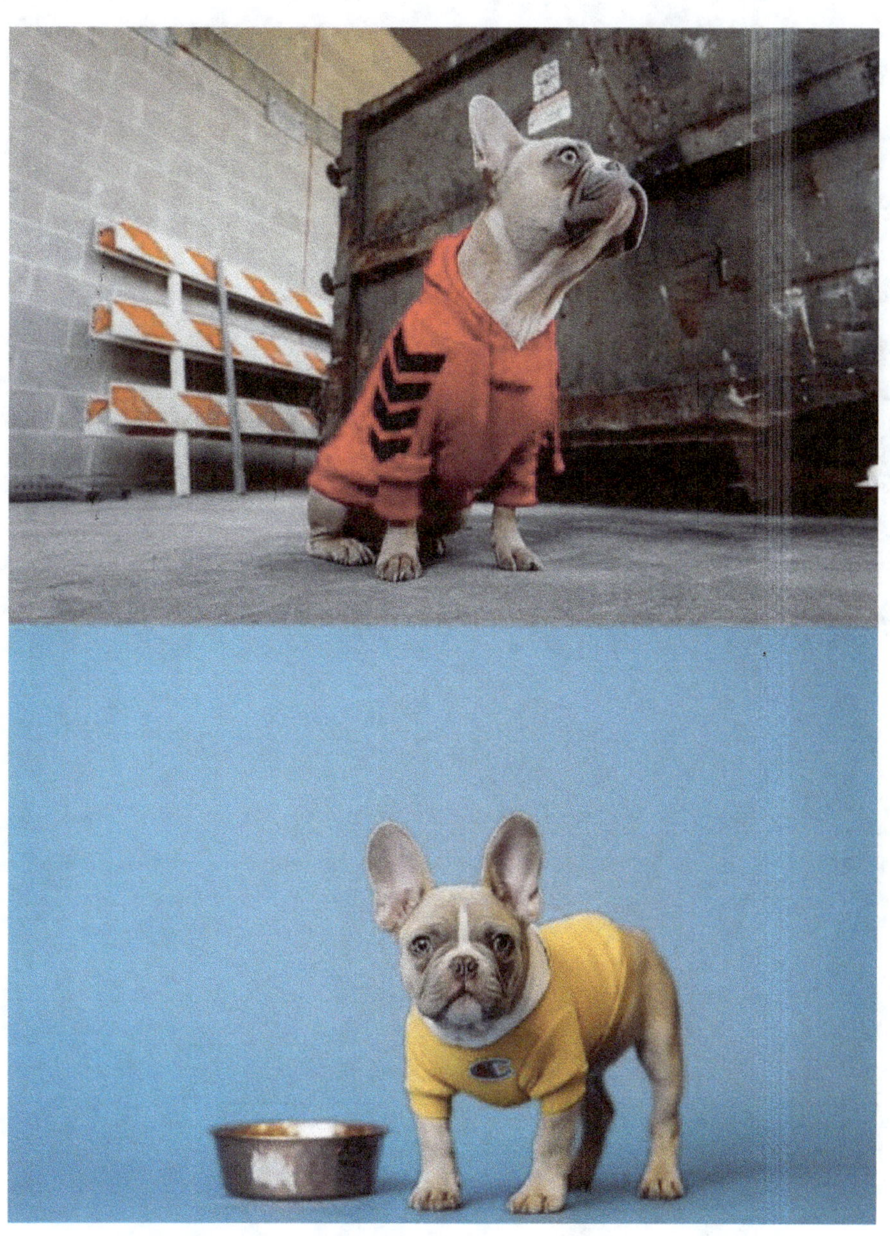

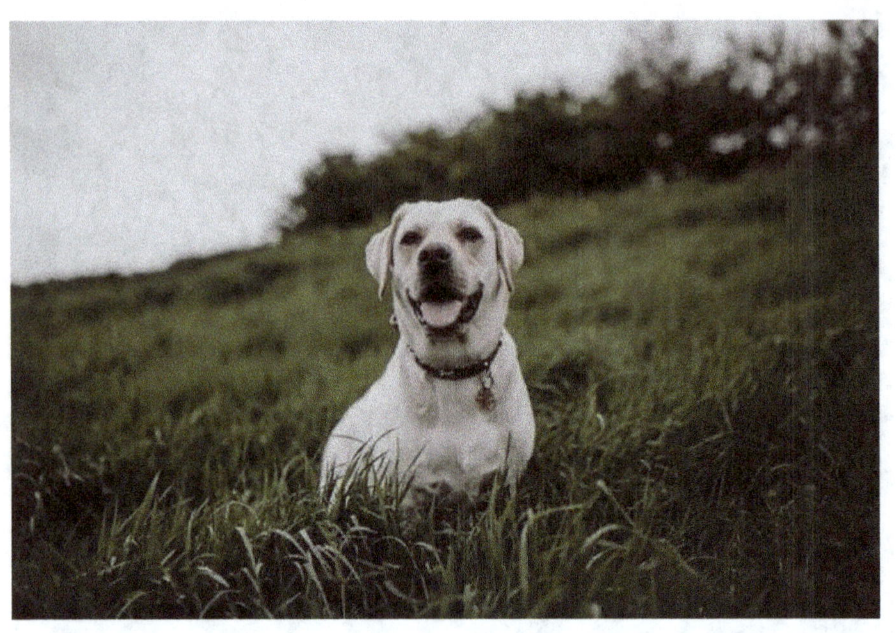

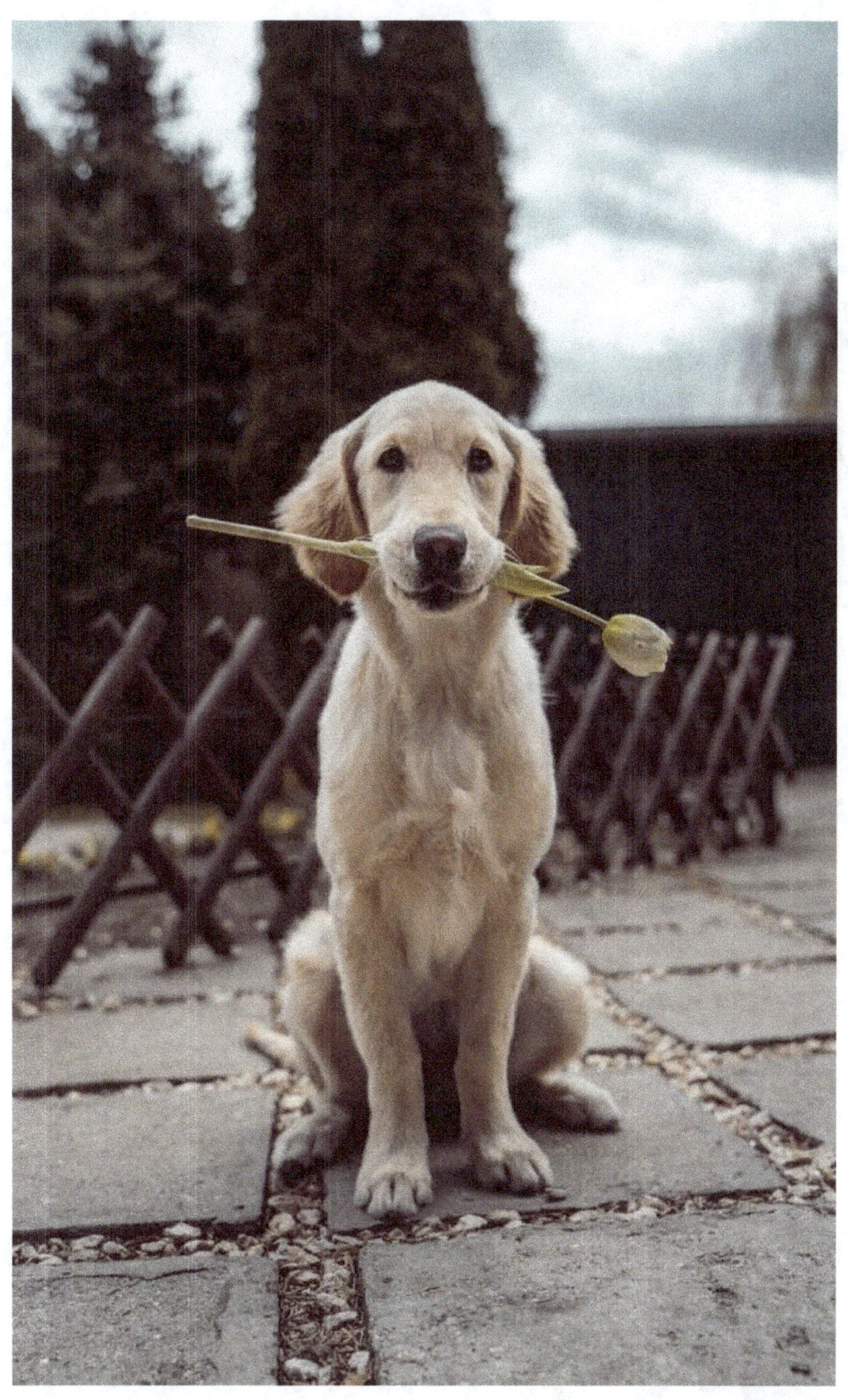

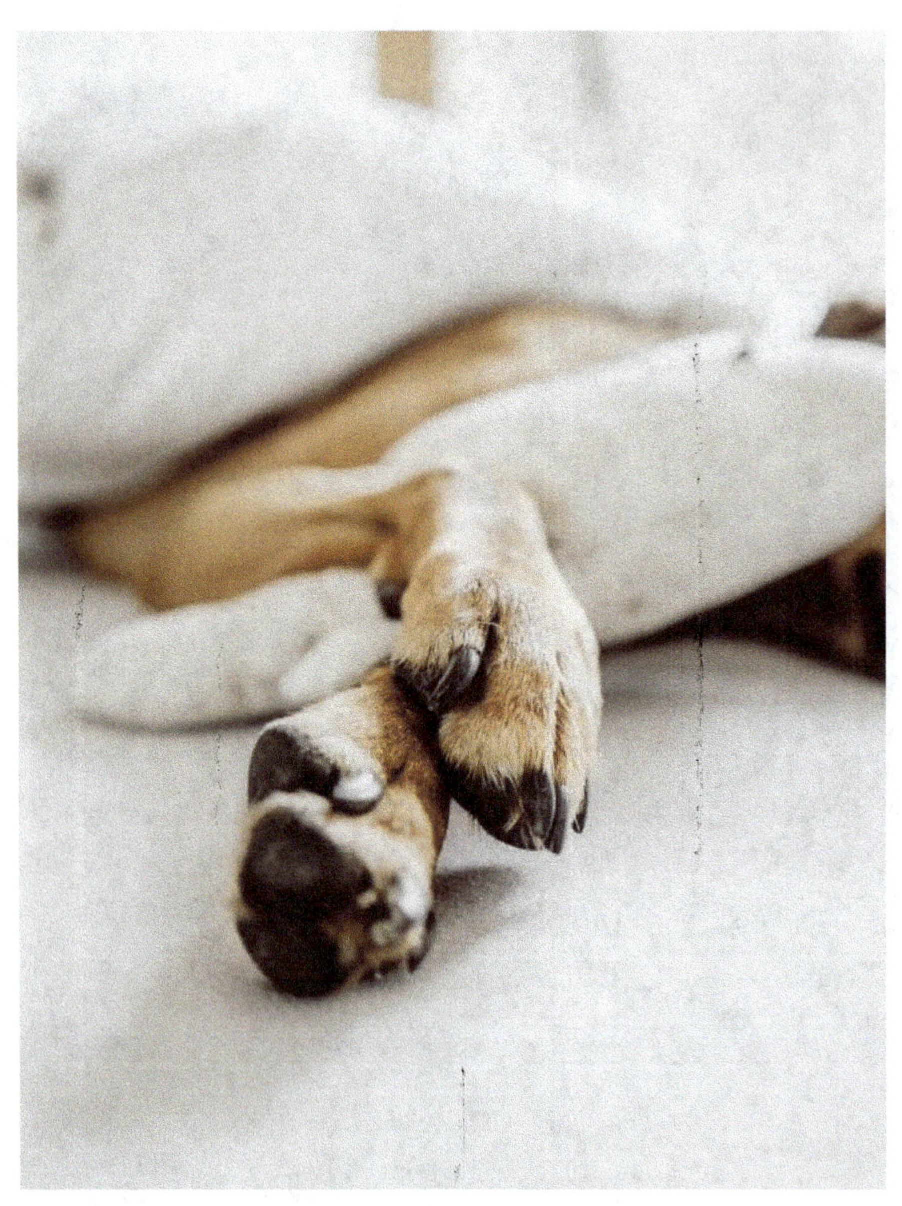

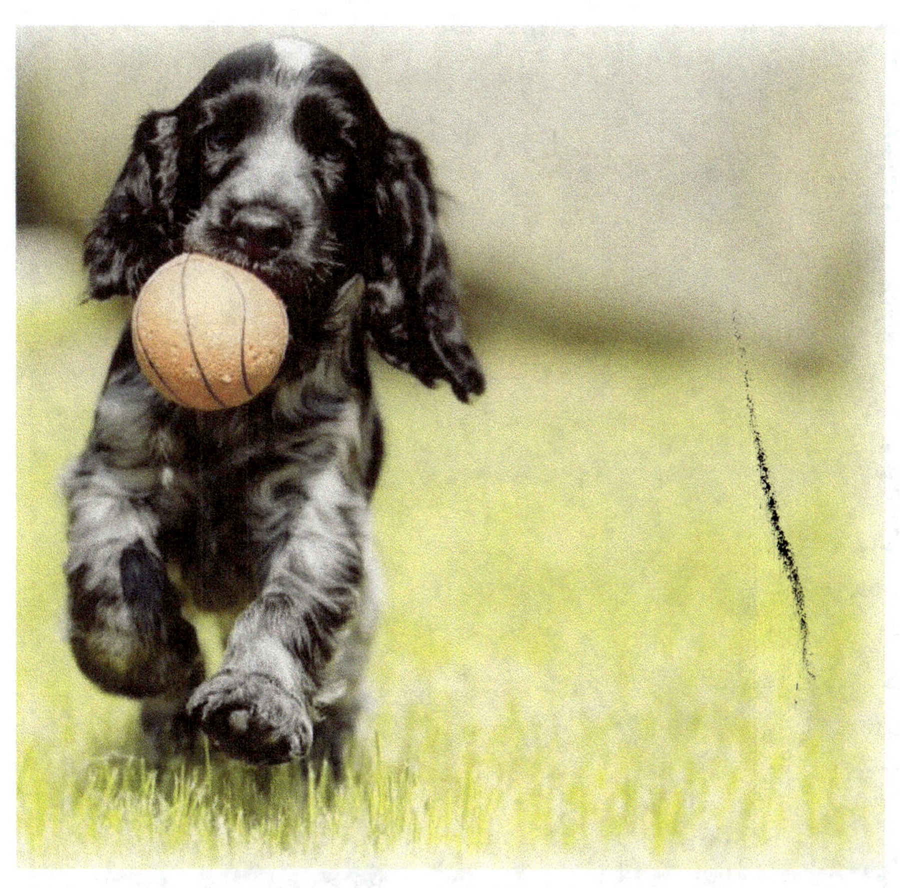

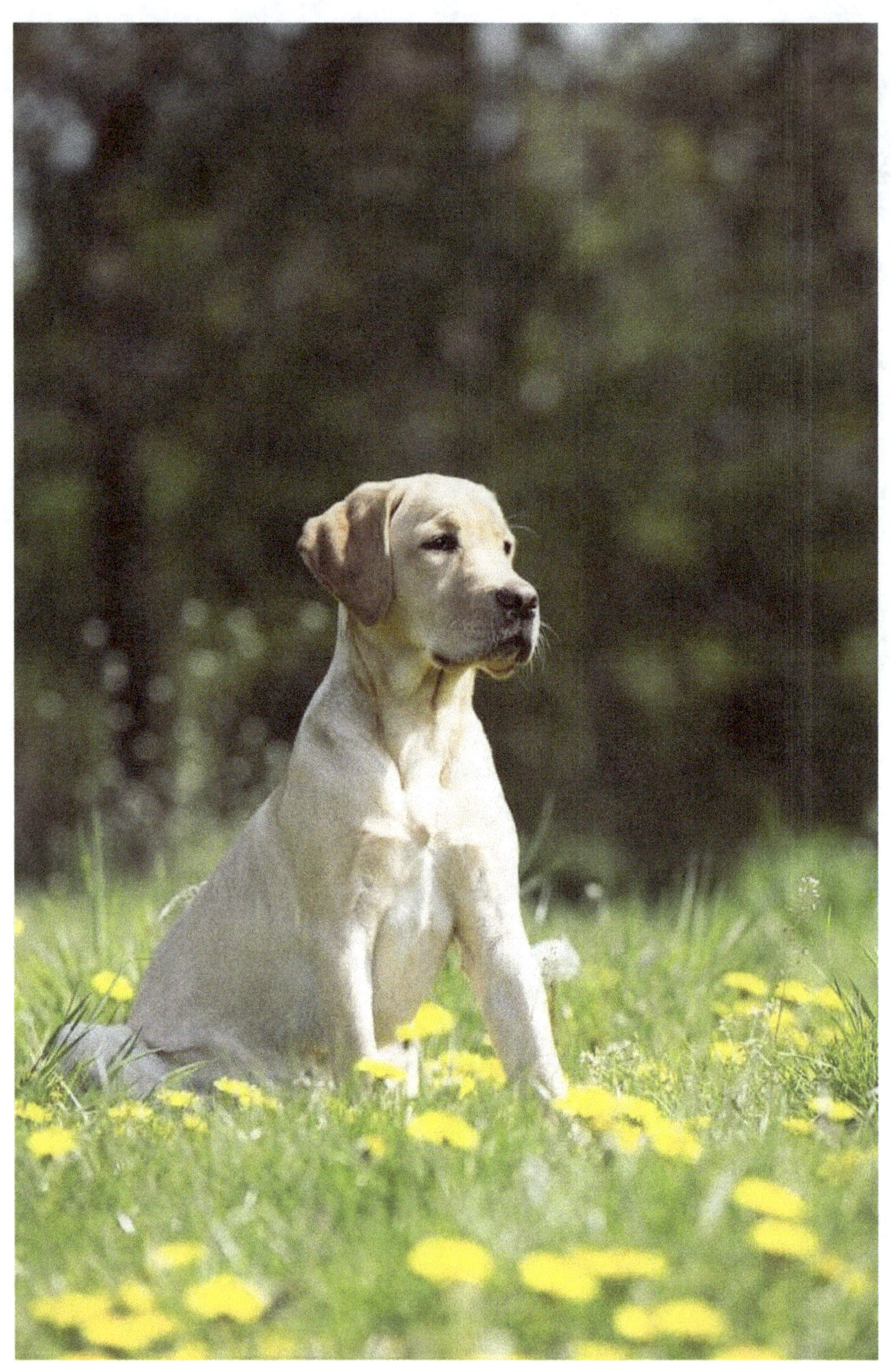

"Dogs love their friends and bite their enemies, quite unlike people, who are incapable of pure love and always have to mix love and hate."

—Sigmund Freud